Eighty-Eight Years
on a Maine Farm

Eighty-Eight Years on a Maine Farm

Will Penney and Minnie Penney

Camden, Maine

Down East Books

An imprint of Globe Pequot, the trade division of
The Rowman & Littlefield Publishing Group, Inc.
4501 Forbes Boulevard, Suite 200,
Lanham, Maryland 20706
www.rowman.com

Distributed by NATIONAL BOOK NETWORK

British Library Cataloguing in Publication Information Available

Library of Congress Cataloging-in-Publication Data Is Available
ISBN 978-1-60893-747-9 (pbk: alk. paper)
ISBN 978-1-60893-767-7 (electronic)

♾️™ The paper used in this publication meets the minimum requirements
of American National Standard for Information Sciences—Permanence of
Paper for Printed Library Materials, ANSI/NISO Z39.48-1992.

To George and Betty and Pamela Penney

who carried on in our old age

And to the hired men who came to this farm

from many parts of the country and

diligently labored to help make it a success

Foreword

By Clarence Day

Kennebec County Farm Agent 1920-1937 and historian of agriculture in Maine

This is more than just another book. It is an invitation by John William Penney (Willie Penney to all who know him) to review with him in retrospect the events of a long and busy life on an active Maine farm. His own recollections and those of his late wife, Minnie Mills Penney, together with excerpts from her diary, will interest the rural sociologist as well as the general reader as they cover a critical period in Maine agriculture.

The Penney farm in Belgrade has been in tne same family for more than one hundred and fifty years. Not only is it an old family farm, it is one of the comparatively few farms whose owners have successfully made the radical change from the self-sufficient agriculture of the nineteenth century to the highly mechanized commercial agriculture of today. Then the farmer raised a little of everything and not much of any one thing. Most of the farm produce — food, fuel, lumber, and even wool for clothing — was used at home. Now practically everything goes to market. Then they produced milk by the quart, now by the bulk tank.

Read carefully and you will see how they made the change. Back in the 'teens Willie was selling some wood for fuel. Then he became interested in good methods of forestry and put them into practice. Soon his woodlot was a leading source of income and as the years went by he had his own sawmill. When he needed the lumber for a new house and a new barn it was there on his own farm. Meantime he had increased his herd of dairy cattle from fifteen or twenty to a hundred or more and had greatly increased milk production per cow.

Turn from dairy to diary and you will get a glimpse of everyday happenings on a busy Maine farm. But busy as the Penneys were, they were not too busy to go to church and grange or take an active part in community and county affairs, or lend a hand to a neighbor in time of need.

In 1943 Minnie Mills Penney was honored by the University of Maine as Outstanding Homemaker. Less than twenty other women in Maine had been so honored then. An Outstanding Homemaker is a person who has been a rural homemaker most or all of her active life, who is recognized by her neighbors as a good housekeeper and homemaker, and who has shown effective leadership in community, county, and state affairs. When you read the citation in her diary you will agree that the requirements were fulfilled. Willie and their son George, who also lives on the old farm, were honored by the Kennebec Extension Association a few years ago as outstanding farmers.

Contents

Minnie Mills Penney
at the time of her marriage in 1909

Will Penney's Memories
of Eight Decades

My first ancestor in Belgrade was George Penney (1755-1814) of Wells. He came to this town in the year 1797, or shortly after that, and settled on lot No. 98 on the east shore of Long Pond near the south end. He bought this property from Samuel Stewart of Belgrade for $250.00 on October 31, 1797. The cellar hole and well of the house of this pioneer Penney can still be seen on the Dunn Road.

George Penney was a Revolutionary War soldier, enlisting on January 10, 1776, in Captain Silas Wild's company in the regiment of Edmund Phinney, and he probably was at Fort George in northern New York with this regiment during the course of the next year. On April 1, 1778, he was mustered at Wells for three years, or during the war, in Captain Merrill's company of Colonel Ebenezer Sprout's regiment, and served as a private, drummer, and sergeant. He was described at West Point on January 1, 1781, as "age 22, 5'8" tall, dark complexioned, dark hair, farmer . . ." He was discharged from the Revolutionary Army on April 1, 1781. At the time of his death in 1814 he was selectman of Belgrade. During this last year of his life, he willed his property to his son, John Penney (1786-1872).

Although there is no document covering the facts, certain obvious reasons existed at that time for the move of George Penney from Wells to Belgrade. It is probable that Samuel

1

Stewart was also from Wells and knowledge of the property would have come through him. George came from a large family and Wells was a very old town even at that time. The Penneys who came to North Belgrade at about this time or shortly before were probably George's brothers. It was the move from the crowded old settlements where opportunities were already occupied to the new frontier where land was available at reasonable prices and a new life could be created.

John Penney, my great-grandfather, was a local shoemaker of Belgrade in the early 1800s, and I still have three pairs of shoes made by him.

After George Penney died in 1814, his widow, Abigail, went back to Wells. From that place in 1835 she made an application for State bounty land in recognition of my great-great grandfather's Revolutionary service.

Reuel Williams, lawyer of Augusta, representative of the Kennebec Proprietors who at one time held title to all Belgrade lands, was a very prominent attorney and businessman in Augusta at this time. After the Kennebec Proprietors sold out their Maine holdings completely in 1816, he purchased a part of them, and did considerable business with Belgrade region people. It is legendary in the Penney family that Reuel Williams loaned my great-great grandfather sufficient money to buy a pair of steers and a horse.

George Penney first put up a house to live in. The cattle were left in the open, and took shelter in the woods in winter and got their feed by browsing at an open stack of hay. Under these weakening conditions, some of the cattle wouldn't make it through the winter. One of the early settlers reported that he once saw six cow hides in one barn, as the result of cows getting "cast."

In 1817, the year of the great exodus from Maine following "eighteen-hundred-and-froze-to-death," John Penney moved from the first Belgrade Penney farm on the Dunn road to the present Penney farm that I have occupied during my life. The original purchase was made from Amos Braley on August 6, 1817, and consisted of the south side of Lot No. 122. The price was one hundred dollars. The place was covered with woods at the time and the original house that I remember may have been a house moved from the Dunn road location. At the time my great-grandfather made this move from the west to the south part of the town, some made disparaging comments about his judgment in moving to this "gulley," as they called it. He placed his first barn on such low ground that he was troubled with water coming in in the spring.

In the original house on this farm good wide boards were used and the cracks were covered with birch bark. At some time an addition was made to the original structure, adding three rooms. This house had three fireplaces, a great brick oven, and an enormous chimney. I have found two places where bricks were made on this farm and I am sure that some of them went into this house. I remember seeing the tracks of a hen made into one of these old farm-made bricks.

The farm house where I was born, built about 1844 by my grandfather and burned to the ground in 1963, had ten rooms, not counting the pantry, and a very large ell. We children had the run of it, except for the parlor, which was never opened, other than on such special occasions as a visit by the minister. In the parlor were the six walnut chairs and the haircloth sofa that had been bought

John Penney (1786-1872), the pioneer on the present farm. Picture taken about 1855.

Mary Mitchell Penney (1794-1879), John's second wife. Picture taken about 1870.

with money saved from boarding the help who were building the railroad through Belgrade in 1848. I peeked in occasionally to find the curtains drawn and the room in darkness.

The back side of the house was shingled with split hemlock shakes that didn't lay close. There was no paper under them, and the plastering being off under the sink, it was so cold in the house some winter mornings that water froze on the kitchen stove. Mother had her own method of fighting the cold. She heated a short hardwood board in the oven and then stood on it while working at the sink.

My grandmother, Hannah Williams Penney (1824-1914), told me that when her father-in-law, John Penney, wanted to do business in Hallowell, he would start from the farm at two o'clock in the morning.

My grandfather, John W. Penney (1819-1892), who died when I was ten years old, was shorter and stouter than my father. He went with a cane and was too feeble in my time to do any work. In this time he read a great deal. But my constant cry of " 'ead, 'ead, Grandpa," must have been a trial to him. He was baldheaded except for a little hair on the back of his neck. One day, carried away by the excitement of the story I had begged to have read to me, I worked my chew of gum into this bit of hair, and it had to be cut off.

Grandfather had an easy-going disposition and was quite religious, reading out of the Bible every morning before breakfast. I don't believe that Grandfather had any of the fine manual skill of his father, John Penney, who was a furniture maker as well as a shoemaker.

Grandfather had six children. I am sure that my father was not his father's favorite son.

Grandfather did tell me one story that gave me quite a scare about the old Penneys of Wells in the eighteenth century. When all kinds of wild animals still roamed the woods in the environs of that town, one of the Penneys was attacked by a pack of wolves while he was cutting wood. By fighting them off with his axe, he managed to get home alive. Probably the purpose of repeating this terrifying tale to me was to keep me from straying into the woods on our farm, something that has happened many times to young children in this neighborhood and other parts of Maine.

John W. (1819-1892) about 1860 and Hannah Williams Penney (1824-1914) about 1875.

About this time I first saw a railroad locomotive at close quarters. This frightened me as much as the wolves of Wells. Father had taken me with him to Belgrade Depot. As he was hitching the horse, a train came into the station from Oakland. Father led me up close to the locomotive. The engine was covered in steam and I could hear the hard pounding of the air pump. Just then a valve blew off with a tremendous blast. If Father hadn't been there to grab hold of, I would have fallen.

The farm, added to in my lifetime and before, now embraces five hundred acres. In the last century nine families lived at some place within the borders of this farm as it is now. At the top of the hill on the right was the home of Charles Chamberlain. On what is called Manley's hill to the southwest—named for Manley Knowles—was the home of Elias Taylor, my grandfather's grandfather. Elias is supposed to have been the first white child born in Augusta in 1762. For many years he preached at the Rockwood Corner church. The next house beyond Manley Knowles' place was the home of Knowlton Penney and his son, Taylor. Beyond that was the home of Asa Axtell and later Melvin Smith. The remains of all these places except that of Chamberlain fall within the borders of the present Penney farm.

5

The first barn built on the Penney farm after 1817 was in a low place across the road from my present house. The first part of the farm that was cleared was on the level part of the top of the hill. I remember the old road that went up to this first field clearing on the north side of a steep hollow.

In the last century there was a road on the east side of the Smith lot that passed through woods and fields and entered the town road halfway through our woods. The first house on that road belonged to John Braley. My Aunt Eliza Penney (1845-1944) told me that she had been in that house many times. Only the cellar hole can be seen today. The next place beyond John Braley's was the home of my grandfather's brother, George Johnson Penney, and later of Judge Greenlief Stevens and Mary Yeaton Stevens. Judge Stevens was well known among Civil War veterans as the commander of Stevens' Battery at Gettysburg and in other memorable campaigns of the Army of the Potomac. His son, Don Stevens, told me that his father once raised two thousand bushels of potatoes, and people came from far and wide to see such a large field so seldom known at that time of subsistence farming. I recall the remains of this place, the barn fallen in and the house moved away. I took the stone out of the cellar in 1908 for the house I planned to build in 1909 and filled the hole up.

About fifty rods north of our present buildings was the home of Sam Judkins. Aunt Eliza told me that Judkins was part Indian, and I believe this to be true. The Judkins barn was moved nearer to our buildings by my grandfather and is now our back barn, called the "Sam barn" by the older people in my family. And in time I filled the Judkins cellar.

The Stevens place, so-called, finally was mortgaged to the bank and my father, J. Newton Penney (1852-1939), got it as a result of a foreclosure.

The particulars of this foreclosure were rather unusual. Elisha Knowles, who had become the owner of this property, had a very cross dog, especially with strangers. One day the dog followed his master's wagon as Elisha drove to Belgrade Depot to visit the store. A villager attempted to put the dog off the store porch and the dog attacked. The man grabbed the dog's ears in an attempt to keep him off, but his wrists were lacerated before a neighbor, shingling on a nearby building, ran up with a hatchet and dispatched the dog. A lawsuit followed and the farm was mortgaged to the Augusta Savings Bank to pay the $600.00 award for injury.

Manley Knowles, our neighbor to the south, moved away when I was quite small, and I can only remember that he used to mow his hay fields with oxen. He had them so well trained that he could ride the mowing machine. His cattle strayed a good deal, which he seemed to think was their right. Manley was a scrappy little fellow, but in an argument with Augustus Brown over the question of his wandering cattle, he came out the worst of it. Brown knocked him down.

Beyond the Knowles place was the home of Taylor Penney, my father's cousin. He suffered very much in his married life from the constant hen-pecking of his wife. The day he was married he lit his cigar with a five dollar bill. That may have been the last happiest day of his life. With the nagging, he was not so prosperous in his later years. I remember when we were milking our cows on one cold winter morning Taylor calling on one of his wife's errands; her cat had gone astray and he was looking for it. Another time, directly after a very severe snow storm and hard blow, his wife decided to go to Belgrade Depot. The roads had not been broken but this made no difference to such a willful woman. Our hill just east of our buildings was drifted full. Father, my brother, Harry (1885-1963), and I had a hard time getting Taylor and his wife through with their horse and sleigh. Their old horse wanted to lay down in the snow. Mary got out in the snow to walk, fretting and fuming, ranting and raving. She finally decided that she was cut out only for life in the city, and obliged Taylor to move to Augusta. They lived for several years in the brick house still standing at the corner of Bridge and State Streets. Their daughter, Lillie Penney (1876-1930), taught school in a building across the street.

The place beyond Taylor's had once been the home of Asa Axtell, a man of civic interest in our community. Notices of Belgrade town meetings were posted at his shop. He built and made the furnishings for the old country school in our neighborhood that I later attended. When I was a boy Mel Smith lived on the Axtell place.

Aunt Eliza remembered being in school here with Mel in the 1850s. He responded to the "western fever" early in life at a time when this ailment was rampant in Maine, and he lived somewhere in the west for a long time in the frontier days. In later life he returned to this neighborhood, and when he had a few drinks would relate tales of his adventures and of his service on a vigilante committee, punctuating the drama of his story with shots from his revolver. On an investigation he was caught alone with desperadoes. Just as the fight was to start, Mel made a spring for the door at the moment one of the bad ones grabbed his coat tails and tore his coat off right under the arms.

Mel could make a plausible case for the role he had played. A game warden took him to Augusta once for fishing in Belgrade Stream in a closed season. After talking with the aged frontiersman at some length, the Judge told him to fish all he wanted to.

Mel had a large pile of manure near his barn, the accumulation of years. I thought of buying it for the back end of the Penney farm, so I went over to see him about it, only to find him in a very bad mood. My next door neighbor had had the same idea and had gone to Mel with an offer. Mel reported, "I caught up a sled stake and said, 'You get out of here. When a man sells his manure, he is selling his farm.' " I had a narrow escape.

One morning Mel came over to see Father, saying that he had been robbed of eighty-five dollars. It seemed that two fellows, one of the Stevens boys and a man named Delaware, had called the night before with a jug of cider. When Mel got up in the morning, he found that his money was missing. He wanted Father to help him go after the suspects, but Father wouldn't do anything. I think he should have helped the old man out. But these fellows sometimes worked for us on the farm, and probably Father didn't want to get mixed up in such an unpleasant situation. Mel had to give up and go home.

Charles Chamberlain lived at the top of the hill on the east of the road. His cellar hole has never been filled. His farm was on top of a hill, poor land, and he was as poor as the land. Charles was very nervous and excitable to an unusual degree. His neighbors used to help his family, with the custom of his paying them back with work. If they didn't call on him in due time, he became very angry. He would put a bushel of corn on his shoulder to be ground and keep it there without taking it off to rest until he had walked to Coombs' Mill in Augusta, seven miles away. He once overtook a team on the way home and he was invited to ride, but after a short distance, he got out, saying that he was in a hurry.

J. Newton (1852-1939) and Celia White Penney (1859-1937) about 1881.

9

Charles had two children, Henry and Mary. Mary was hired to look after my Aunt Eliza when she went to school for the first time about 1851. Henry got a gun and this made his father very worried and nervous when he went hunting. If Henry fired in hearing distance, his father would shout, "Have you shot yourself?" and start to run in the direction of the sound.

Part of the Penney farm is on the south end of the great gravel esker extending intermittently many miles to the north left by the glacier ten or twenty thousand years ago. Penney Pond, about twenty-five acres in extent, is the largest of a group of sixteen glacial ponds in the immediate vicinity, one of the most interesting and conspicuous geological wonders in the State of Maine. These ponds were made by gigantic blocks of glacier ice becoming submerged and buried for many years beneath the soil debris carried by the glacier. Thawing out after many years, when the glacier had receded, the ice left a deep pothole that remained filled with water from supplies in the surrounding terrain. Some of these glacier ponds make almost a perfect circle.

Of course we were unaware of the geological history when we were learning to swim in Penney Pond. A point narrows the pond in one place and there may be a spring there as it is always the last place to freeze over. The beach at the north end is not good for it drops off into deep water abruptly, but at the south end the shore could not be better.

There is a time at freezeup and shortly after before the ice is covered with snow when a considerable noise comes from the expanding ice and movements of water below, a kind of rumbling and groaning sound. My cousin, Fred Brown, didn't care for this rather ominous sound, and he didn't like to go near the ponds at that time of the year.

When I was a very small boy I remember a day when I was helping Father mend fence near the house. A neighbor stopped and told him that Ulysses S. Grant had just died. This was in the month of July, 1885, and I was only a little more than three years old. Of course I hardly knew what our neighbor was talking about. But something about the manner of the announcement stayed with me, and I never forgot this time of the passing of one of the more memorable Americans of the last century. General

10

Grant had special significance in that time and place. Belgrade was literally sprinkled with men who had served under Grant in the Army of the Potomac and some had seen him when the Army marched on Pennsylvania Avenue only twenty years before. He was one of the few important Americans of the time that local country people could feel a special kinship with.

In those early times eighty and more years ago, Ellen Knowles (1858-1919) was our nearest neighbor, and she and Mother were close friends. Many-a-time I recall trudging along across the field, holding Mother's hand, going for a visit. Ellen always took us into the parlor where I much admired the well-kept furniture, and believed our neighbor must be very rich.

Now that splendid old house, that dates from early in the 1800s, is coming to a sad end, much in disrepair, with some of the panes in the windows fallen out.

I have a recollection of one early Christmas sometime in the late 1880s. Harry and I had heard a good deal about the character and doings of Santa Claus, that he only visited good children. We made an effort to be worthy. The house chimney ran down beside our room and the night before that Christmas we slept very little, hoping to hear Santa Claus when he descended through it. We heard nothing, as it happened, and doubts crept over us. But when dawn first broke over the farm, we rushed down stairs in our nightdresses and found that he had been there. He had filled stockings with popcorn, peanuts, candy and oranges. On the mantle we found games and picture books. Dinah, the big doll, had been rehabilitated with a new dress and a new eye. From then on we were firm believers in Santa Claus.

Perhaps realizing that I had a lot to learn, or to get me out from under foot, my formal schooling started a year earlier than was usual at that time. I entered school in the neighborhood in the month of September in the year 1887. And I remember well on my arrival at the schoolhouse my deep humiliation at being seated among the girls.

In those days it was common for the teachers to be young men or women who had been brought up and lived in the immediate neighborhood. My first teacher, lived with her folks half a mile up the road. They were all terrified in a thunderstorm.

11

I remember the first big one that struck when she was teaching in our little school. She dismissed the school immediately and led the stampede for home with tremendous power of foot. I was the last one off, making as much noise as I could at the top of my voice.

My first lesson was based on the word "cat," which kept me busy for a long time. Good behavior brought its reward, and I was soon promoted to switch cutter. The big boys started to notice me then, telling me where I could cut the larger sticks, which they said they recommended.

There was a little mouse that used to come out on the floor when school was in session and the students were quiet. We called him "teacher's mouse" and everyone loved the little creature. One day Harry hit him on the head with his lead pencil and he went rolling and tumbling down the aisle to the teacher's feet. Soon he recovered enough to find his hole, but we didn't see him again for several days.

At that time in Belgrade, as in the rest of Maine, the old school district law was still in force. Each little neighborhood in all of our country towns was a power unto itself and, in the most direct democracy on the face of the earth, initiated and operated schools. On infrequent occasions a town supervisor might call to inspect the work of the teacher and the children. I recall such an instance when the supervisor was visiting and a small boy was reading at the teacher's knee, with greater confidence than ever before, at last shouting, "Take off your thumb." This performance attracted the supervisor's attention, as he said to the eager little boy, "That is a pretty suit you have." "Yes," the little boy replied, "And we didn't pay for it."

Some boys found a large hornets' nest and they hid it in the schoolroom one cold morning. The first hornet that warmed up and came out didn't attract much attention, but then they came in full force, and there was a riot. There were many casualties and some started for home, but the teacher sent the larger boys to bring them back to the battlefield. The war on the hornets went on with the use of shingles until the room was cleared of them. As so many of us nursed our wounds, the teacher seemed to think we had suffered enough for our wrongdoing. She did not see fit to mete out further punishment, which might have been justified.

There was a wonderful hill for coasting near our school house and we made good use of it. A man living in a house at the top of this hill could play the violin, and one day he brought it down to us. It was the first time I had heard a violin. I never forgot this sweet music.

In this same house lived the Widow Newell with her large family of children, which she ruled with an iron hand. George, one of the boys about my age, having been up to some mischief that had immediately come to his mother's knowledge, thought if he brought me home as a visitor, his mother would be forced to overlook it. His stratagem didn't work; she went at him with a barrel stave, and I fled the scene with his yells ringing in my ears.

A person going by this place observed the Widow Newell hoeing alone in her garden. He said to her, "You need a man." She answered, "I've got the poison already for him!"

At last the family on the hill near the school moved away and we had the run of an old orchard where there was a very large pear tree that sometimes bore. It was in a rich place and one year it was full. Our interest increased as we observed the pears ripening. At last the day was set for me and all of my young friends to bring baskets and bags and a fair division would be made. On the appointed morning we all arrived at the pear tree only to find it stripped. There are no words to describe our rage and disappointment.

Several of the big boys in my school had already learned to chew tobacco, a very common practice for men in those days. We younger boys looked on at these mannerisms in admiration and hoped that soon we could also acquire the habit with its attendant arts. One night on the way home these boys made us very happy by giving each of us a large piece of chewing tobacco. Soon this softened and swelled in our mouths and propped them open. We couldn't spit, but we could swallow and we were overcome with joy. We were learning to chew. This pleasure was very short-lived. Before we had gone far on the road for home a terrible nausea and dizziness collapsed us in the ditch. Here we rolled and retched in agony, thinking that we had come to our end. After

13

raising a quantity of that awful juice, we were barely able to get to our feet and continue towards home, trembling, tottering, and faltering along without hats or dinnerpails.

There was one boy in particular who made a lot of trouble in school in time. He was the one that had surprised the supervisor in his early days. Occasionally he had to be called up by the teacher to be straightened out. He loved to fight, and I had many scraps with him, not always friendly ones. One night the school scholars started off for home as usual, but we stayed to throw rocks, and I happened to hit him near the temple with a sharp scaler. He went into the air like a jumping-jack and started for home at top speed. Far ahead the other scholars that had gone on before stood in the road to watch him run. I had hardly reached home when his mother arrived at our door with a team bringing Fred done up in a sheet stained with much blood. I fully expected severe consequences, but nothing happened. It was ten days before we saw Fred again and the look on his face did not indicate that I was forgiven for almost committing mayhem.

Of course I wanted Fred to forget his injury, so I invited him home after school on one occasion to go sailing on my raft. When we got out in the middle of the Bog pond, I told him that here it was supposed to have no bottom. Still filled with the spirit of vengeance, he chose this place to push me off the raft. He was still clinging to his hurt.

One cold winter day when we arrived at school we found the door open and the windows all gone. The term was finished out at my home, where the teacher boarded, as it happened. Fred was the only one in our school who didn't join us, and we suspected him of stealing the windows and perhaps even stripping the pear tree.

When I was about seven years old, Father was putting a new forty foot addition on the end of the old barn. It was first necessary to split the old part and move the front out six feet to widen the tieup, which had been too narrow. Once some blocking gave way, and the part being moved almost fell over.

The carpenter, George Wade, was a hard-swearing man during the day, but his tales of his personal adventures thrilled me in the evening. I believed all of those stories then and perhaps they

14

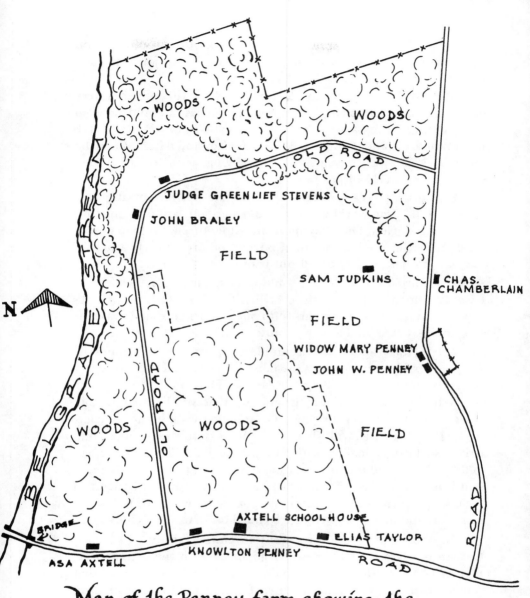

Map of the Penney farm showing the various families who lived within its present borders about one hundred years ago.

The maps and drawings for this book were done by Anthony Vajs of Mt. Vernon, Maine, young master in the graphic arts.

were true. In those days occasional help like this would stay on the farm boarding and rooming with us until the job was completed.

Mr. Wade had gone to sea earlier in his life under a very brutal captain. I remember him saying, "At last I could take no more and, grabbing a codfish, I laid the captain on the deck. He was carried off and I didn't see him for several days. When he came back he was a changed man, having acquired what one would call a lovely disposition."

Perhaps Mr. Wade's least plausible tale was of working in a powder mill. The working crew would sit about at noon smoking and telling stories. One, having lit his pipe, threw his match over his shoulder, where it set a bin of powder on fire. Nearly a bushel was burned before they could put it out.

It seemed to me that if I could only swear as Mr. Wade did, I would somehow have a more brilliant future. On my first rehearsal Mother boxed my ears with such violence that I was unable to cry for as much as a minute.

After Harry and I had accumulated quite a bit of money in our piggy banks, unknown to the family, we cleaned them out and ran away to the store at Belgrade Depot. Here we laid out all of our savings on candy. The large amount that we obtained for our money was at first very pleasing. On the long walk home we commenced to fear what Mother and Father would say upon our arrival so heavily loaded with our purchases. We did what we could to lessen the quantity of candy on the way. Quite a bit was said when we arrived and the store keeper was roundly condemned for taking advantage of children. As for us, we were given doses of castor oil and our great adventure ended on that melancholy note.

In those days we always went to church at the Rockwood Corner as a family. Father would go ahead with the big carriage, taking Grandmother and Grandfather. I followed in another wagon with the rest of the family. I would hold Sandy in until we were far behind, and then let him go to catch up. I had gotten acquainted with Sam Spaulding, a boy of my own age. Instead of attending the sermon, we stayed outside on one Sunday and told stories as we sat under the hitch rail. That was probably the first time we had sinned.

16

Penney farm buildings, 1928.

We had many dogs. The first one was little Trim, a rabbit beagle, whose whole life was devoted to the chase. One night, after a hard day in the woods, he had fallen asleep under the end of the stove. All at once he commenced to tremble and yelp loudly. He was dreaming about trailing in the woods. Years after Trim we had an even smaller dog, Che-Che. He became famous on the Penney farm for clearing the fields of woodchucks. He didn't dig them out but instead would conceal himself near the hole and lie in wait for them. He was known to get as many as three wood-chucks in one day.

Once when Harry and I came home from the little school, Mother told us that the men had gone to the woods to dig out a fox that had been robbing our hen roost. We promptly hurried out to the north end of Fox Hill where we soon saw a mother fox and five little ones playing around a hole. We found the men at another hole, digging where they had found feathers. They came back with us, and dug out the five little foxes, and we took them home. We gave one to a neighbor girl who had come from school with us, putting it in a bag for her to take it home. Her father had other ideas; when he learned that she had a small wild animal in the bag he struck it on the door rock to kill it.

Harry and I put our four in a big wooden box, nailing stout slats across the top, and all in vain; the mother fox came sometime that night, gnawed the slats to get at the little foxes, and took them away with her.

17

Animals were not used as well in those days as now, and we had a number of incidents with dogs that had turned ugly under cruel treatment in the neighborhood of our farm. A neighbor was once mowing with a hand scythe in a field near our house, when he was attacked by an ugly dog. Holding the dog off with the scythe, he backed away until he reached the yard of our house where Mother was standing outside. Frightened by this scene, she ran into the house for protection, and our hired man shot the dog on the spot.

My brothers and I were as much interested in woodchucks as the dogs were, catching them in traps at first and later shooting them. For this we had an old musket that we loaded with a ball wrapped in a rag to fit the bore and hold the ball in place. Some body asked, "Why do you use the cloth in loading?" Justin (1888-1938), my little brother, replied, "So it won't hurt the animal." At last we got a better gun.

Woodchucks feed mostly early in the morning and towards night. Going on a long hunt one afternoon, I made a record for this farm by shooting six within the given time. The woodchuck has poor eyesight. One day while cultivating beans, I saw one far out in the field. On sensing me, he started for his refuge in the woods at top speed. As I happened to be right in his old road, he bumped into the cultivator. And they can be eaten. I knew of two families in the neighborhood who made a practice of dining on them on occasion.

In the spring and fall we trapped skunks, much to Mother's dismay. Father offered to show us how to skin the first one we caught. When he made a careless cut, he stopped and threw down the knife. Later when we went in to the house we found him trying to wash up, with rags burning on the stove to neutralize the odor.

We had a good shore on Belgrade Stream for fishing. We built a boat that was of great use to us. With it we could spear at night, using a torch made of a ball of rags soaked in kerosene on the end of a stick. Landing a big eel was not much fun.

Smoking the hams from the hogs on the farm in the early spring was an interesting chore. The hams were hung on hooks suspended from the top of a large barrel. The smoke kettle was a broad, shallow pan placed inside. Into this live coals were placed, dry corn cobs were tiered on top of the coals, with the coals covered with sawdust, leaving no vents for air. Then the barrel with the hams was placed over the smoker, with old blankets tied over the barrel to keep the smoke in. In this way one smoke would last all day.

We were smoking hams on one occasion when Will Knowles, a neighbor, was going by. He noticed much more smoke than was usual around the barrel and gave the alarm. The barrel was afire. I came running and found Father shoveling in snow as fast as he could. Usually for a finished ham several smokes are necessary, but in this case the one was enough.

Father kept a flock of sheep, a necessity on our farm from the beginning. They were always pastured on the east side of the road in an area that is now grown up but was then many acres of good pasture. One year dogs killed several of them, severely chewing another that we managed to bring back by doctoring at the house. Years later some sheep that Father bought turned out to have a disease that caused the wool to peel off. He sold them all at that time, ending the sheep business on the Penney farm.

In 1887, when I was five years old, Father bought a fifty acre tract of land in the adjacent town of Rome, where we pastured the young cattle and dry cows for thirty-eight years. It was in a corner formed by the main road back of Long Pond and a cross road north of Yallaly Hill. As soon as Harry and I were big enough to stand the trip, we would help drive the cattle to this pasture. We always did our driving on Saturday. This pasture was thirteen miles from our farm and we looked forward to the driving day as surpassing the Fourth of July.

There were about one hundred and fifty rock maples on this pasture and we decided to tap them. We built a nice camp in the pasture and made a fireplace about five feet square for two large pans containing the sap to be boiled down to syrup. Harry and I, with Mother along to keep house, would go to the camp in March and stay for the sap running season. At this time syrup sold for one dollar a gallon. We made a lot of it and enjoyed our spring expeditions to the Rome pasture and sap orchard for about six years.

I remember one year on the first night in camp a late winter snow storm came on with a violent wind. I woke up about midnight to find that a little crack in the wall had let in snow and Harry's head was in a snowdrift. A squirrel had bored into our straw tick, but we didn't blame him for refusing to stay out on such a wild night. Harry managed to shoot him a few days later, when he was tapping a tree. Squirrels know how to get a sort of syrup and sugar by gnawing the bark on the small limbs of the rock maple so that the bark will run down and dry for them to consume later.

On one occasion we lost about ten gallons of syrup, a serious loss. There had been a big run of sap in the day, and we had been boiling in the evening, leaving the pans full overnight with the fire not just right; it was all spoiled.

When I was going to Cony High School about 1900 and Mother planned for me to help her in the sap orchard for several spring weeks, I became a very popular boy. Every boy and girl in Cony wanted to go with me.

When I was about ten years old and we had just started the haying, we put in our first small load in great haste and too green, as a shower threatened. Because of the condition of the hay, we pitched off at once and spread it out thinly over a large scaffold. The shower passed and as soon as it stopped raining, I went into the barnyard just at the moment when there came a flash of lightning and an earsplitting crash. The barn had been struck. In the barnyard where I stood, I felt a compression of the air as if a door had closed upon one quickly in a closet. The horses came tearing out of the barn, as they had not been unharnessed or hitched. A small fire started right in the new hay, but the men soon put it out. A blackening of the wood can be plainly seen in the barn where this occurred. A post supporting the collar beam in the barn was slivered with the end of one splinter driven through the roof of the barn between the boards. Directly below in the tieup the links of a tiechain were welded together.

Many years ago we lost two cows in the home pasture, probably killed by lightning. An ox in our Rome pasture was killed by lightning, reported to us by the caretaker. In 1953 a large heifer, due to freshen soon, was killed by lightning. Some years previous to this lightning struck a knoll on the farm, tearing up the ground as if a large stump had been lifted out.

Later it was recognized that the common practice of my father's time of selling the hay from Maine farms and putting nothing back in the ground tended to run a farm down. During this period I can remember two pressing crews coming to our farm with a stationary hay bailer or, "press," and checking off the bale weights as they were loaded.

Three jobs kept us busy on the farm most of the winter: hauling the ice from Belgrade Stream to our ice house, transporting the barn manure to distant fields on the horse sled to be spread in the spring, and cutting and sawing up the wood with the bucksaw. Once working up a hollow-hearted beech with a crosscut saw, we heard a rattling sound, a section of the tree fell apart, and a squirrel popped out leaving a peck of good beechnuts behind.

Father once brought home a molasses hogshead and sawed it in half in the kitchen. A lot of brown sugar was left inside, and we helped to clean it out. Half of this hogshead was used in the barnyard for a watering trough, and we never got tired of playing around it.

One day Harry fell into the water in the half hogshead, and the hired man had to pull him out and carry him to the house. I followed along wondering if Harry would die from this immersion.

In my earliest days all of the water came from a well at the lower end of the barnyard, and there was a pipe from this to the house. It was not a very satisfactory arrangement. Coming from school we would bring our dinner pails full of water from the spring.

A chain pump furnished water for the stock which Harry and I used to take care of much of the time, when Father was working in the fields or woods. It was impressed upon us that it was a great sin to let the hogshead get empty.

In 1896 Father decided to draw water from an old well in a low part of the field sixty rods away from the buildings. Father bought and we placed a small windmill near the well and with

21

this pumped to the barn. This arrangement was only partially satisfactory, as the windmill was small and not in a place where wind currents commonly struck it. So we were sometimes out of water in the winter and the cattle had to be driven to the well through deep snow and water bailed out for them. And sometimes we would go a half mile to the end of the road where there is a brook. A neighbor also watered his cattle in the brook and when the herds got mixed difficulties arose. Many years later, I put a one horsepower gas engine in place to use when the wind would not blow the mill.

We kept several hogs on the manure under the barn. By scattering corn on the pile they kept it rooted away from the scuttles. Getting out the manure in the spring became a very hard job when Father got to putting whole shocks of corn down for the hogs. The unconsumed stocks would bind the pile together making it almost impossible to pitch out. It was a poor practice. A neighbor boy lost his watch down the scuttle. A hog met him with the fob in his mouth. The remains of the watch were found in the spring.

These primitive arrangements didn't make for big milk production, but our cows were not of a dairy breed, and most of them were dry in the winter. Durham was the principal strain in our cattle, an old utility and beef breed, and we raised many steers. We usually sold these for about six cents per pound dressed, sometimes more, sometimes less.

We had plenty of ox yokes on the farm at that time of all necessary sizes, and Harry and I had great fun breaking the young steers. I used to haul logs to Wings' Mill with one pair. Once we got stuck on the railroad tracks that crossed the road half way to the Mill. By working snow under the runners we got away with logs and steers intact. On this route at another time we had to stop at Andrew Dudley's to get some ox shoes replaced. Once that operation was over, the steers decided to take their head and return immediately to the Penney farm without delivering the logs. I couldn't do anything with them. Seeing my plight, Andrew took charge and with the free use of the goad stick and brad managed to restore their will to continue the trip to the Mill.

22

We kept an average of rather less than thirty head of live-stock, two or more hogs, a small flock of hens, which had the run of the barnyards, and almost always some turkeys.

The pasture was poor and nothing was ever done to improve it. Father did not believe in sowing clover, haying was always late and the hay of poor quality. Most of the cows freshened in the spring, the milk being made into cheese, my grandmother making this her special work for many years. Most of the cheese was sold in Oakland, and one of the first trips away from the farm was going to Oakland with my father and a wagon load of cheese. This would have been about 1885.

Calves had enough skim milk or whey to get a good start but little or no grain.

Grandmother Hannah was a very industrious woman, always busy on the farm.

During the Civil War Grandmother made uniforms for the Union Army. She had an early "Weed" sewing machine that I believe she used in this work. I remember a few of the long blue coats and the brass buttons stored here on the farm, leftovers from this project. She made butter in the winter and cheese in summer.

In winter there was much less milk production but what there was we placed in deep, broad pans for the cream to rise to the top. This method, of rising the cream in deep cans set in tanks of ice water, was utilized from the earliest times until the development and distribution of the cream separator to the larger farms. Of course the separator was a much more efficient method, but the farm hogs didn't do so well on the skim milk left over from the process.

We had a barrel churn and the task of turning the crank often fell to me, a tedious job if the butter "wouldn't come."

One day when the butter had "come," Grandmother went to the barrel churn and unfastened the top. Just at that moment a traveling agent knocked at the door and Grandmother started to answer the call, when somebody behind her gave the churn crank a turn and the whole contents went on the floor through the opened top. With her long, voluminous skirts Grandmother filled the door and concealed the mess from the caller and dismissed him in a hurry.

Grandmother's cheese-making was much more interesting. We still have the big, brass kettle for the milk to begin this process. It was necessary to have "runnet" to curdle the milk. I used to go across the field to a neighbor butcher, Nate Knowles, for the stomach of a calf that he would have waiting for me stretched on a crotched stick. The stomach contains a substance that has the effect of making the milk curdle. A little water that the stomach was soaked in would turn the milk. Then the curd had to be broken up and the whey strained out of it through cheese cloth. While this process was going on a few bits had to be thrown to Jim, my tame crow, to keep him away from the work.

The curd was then put in hoops seven inches high and sixteen inches in diameter. Two of these would be placed in the two presses that we had. After pressing they would usually stand up and hold together alright. Occasionally one had to be wrapped with a cloth band, and after removing from the press they had to be greased and turned every day. By these careful means Grandmother's cheese was of the highest quality.

Grandmother was much displeased on one occasion when Father returned from Oakland after delivering a load of her cheese with the report that the storekeeper was selling cheese from a number of other suppliers under her name.

There is no bird that can be so easily tamed as a crow. My crow was always on hand, and would go to the fields with us. He was so domesticated that if other crows flew over, he would become so frightened that he would dive into the grass.

We had a little black dog at this time and the crow and the dog were enemies. One day they engaged in physical combat, with the crow getting away to a tree with the loss of a few feathers and a bit of skin. From the security of his perch he proceeded to scold our black dog in crow language.

Another of Grandmother's special chores was the making of soft soap. We usually commenced the year with a full barrel. First she would set up the leach barrel with some straw in the bottom and the rest filled with wood ashes over a board with channels leading to a pan in front of the barrel. She would turn a pail of water on the ashes every day until she got all the lye she needed. The lye was boiled with the accumulated fat from the hog carcasses and other fatty remains from farm butchering. The new soft soap was put in the soap barrel with whatever was left over from the previous year. The soap barrel was in the shed and Grandmother in going by would often stop and give it a stir with a long-handled paddle kept for that special purpose.

When Grandmother Hannah married my grandfather in the 1840s, her stepbrother, Alfred Williams, born in Waterville in 1826, and two years younger than Grandmother, came here to the farm with her, worked on the farm, and attended the Axtell School, where I went many years later.

Uncle Alfred was the true adventurer. Sometime in the late 1840s he left the farm to work in Boston. At the time of the first gold rush in 1849, he made his way to California. Upon his return to these parts in 1851 to marry Mary Jane May, the daughter of Captain John May, veteran of the war of 1812, he romantically presented his bride with a wedding ring made from a nugget of California gold.

Uncle Alfred's interest in travel was never-ending. He went to Cuba as a construction engineer for the Baldwin Locomotive Works. In Cuba he became interested in dentistry and studied the science and obtained a degree to practice. This became his real life work after his many early adventures. He became well known in Philadelphia for his established dental practice in the later decades of the 1800s. Uncle Alfred was very inventive, and he devised many appliances for the dental profession. By 1900 he had crossed the Atlantic twenty times, probably in connection with the dental profession and his inventions.

Uncle Alfred came here to the farm a number of times in his later life, in the first years after I was married, to spend some time with Grandmother amid the scenes of his youth. When he was eighty-six he carved his initials on a birch tree that stood at the top of the

25

hill easterly from Grandmother's house, and he remarked at this time that "this tree stands on the land where I plowed and harrowed 70 years ago; as a souvenir I inscribe my name and date of my visit 23 Aug 1912." On the same day he had his picture taken beside the door of the Axtell school commenting "this is the old school house where I graduated, not from books, but with my gun and my fishing hook."

The land kept in hay was only a half or a third of what we have now, and we rotated it very slowly, plowing up only a few acres each year, perhaps two or three for potatoes and four or five for corn, allowing this to ripen on the stalk and husking it in evenings in the barn. Father always had a pair of rather cheap horses and often a pair of oxen. I thinked he liked the oxen best. One hired man seemed to be enough except in busy times.

In one of my father's account books, I find the following figures covering the size of the Penney farm, under date of December 13, 1897:

	Acres
Home place	128
Judkins place—1	59
Braley lot	56
Judkins—2	58
Farrow lot	25
	326
Home lot about	50
Lot no. 114 about	125
Total acres	501

The sale of the Rome pasture in 1926 and the lot across the road reduced the farm by about one hundred and ninety acres. I have added to this reduced figure so that the farm now stands at about 400 acres.

Father was a rather thick-set man of more than average strength, weighing about 185 pounds. My uncle, George Penney (1861-1943), once remarked about Father, "It took a good man

Uncle Alfred Williams at eighty-six, by the door of the old Axtell school and his tree on the farm, August 23, 1912

27

to follow him with a scythe." Father worked hard but he was not very successful. He liked to build and repair the buildings and clear up new land, but his fields were low in productivity and run out.

Father employed extra help only in a busy season, not on a full time basis. Jim Bartlett was one of Father's hired hands that we had on the farm for a season about 1892. He was a good worker but with a weakness for liquor.

A circus was coming to Augusta and we were all planning to go. On that day Jim had the cows milked, the chores all done and his best suit on in good season, obviously "raring to go." Father drove us to Augusta in the two-seated wagon in time to watch the exciting circus parade through the streets. After the parade I went back to the wagon where I found Jim already drunk and trying to force a fight on a neighbor of ours, Emery Knowles, who was trying to back away from him and laugh him off. Before the day was over Jim was taken in by the Augusta police and locked up. While two of them were leading him across the river bridge to the jail, he had brought his arms behind them suddenly and brought their heads together with a smart crack. Jim didn't get back to the farm for a week.

I think that Father and Mother were unusual for country families in subscribing to three papers, the *Lewiston Journal,* with Republican leanings in those days, the *Zion's Advocate,* and the *Maine Farmer.* The last was initiated and edited for many years by Ezekiel Holmes (1801-1865) of Winthrop, called the Father of Maine Agriculture by my friend, Clarence Day, who has written his biography, a twentieth century successor to Holmes as an agricultural publicist.

Our library of books was small. We were well supplied with Bibles and hymn books, a copy of *Uncle Tom's Cabin, Pilgrims' Progress,* two volumes of a life of Daniel Boone, and one of Stanley's books on Africa. Later we took the *Youths' Companion.* I now find that I have accumulated on the farm eight hundred volumes.

In 1898 I entered Cony High School in Augusta. The principal at that time was Frederick Cook, a gifted educator and stern disciplinarian. He later was principal of a much larger high school in Manchester, New Hampshire.

To get acquainted with the entering class, Cook would teach a period or two in science. Then leaving us with some problem to work on, he would walk through the corridors inspecting the other classes at work. During his absence we would sometimes take the opportunity to visit the store across the road from the school.

Once returning from his corridor inspections unexpectedly, Cook caught Robert Partridge playing at a window of our classroom. Quickly stepping up to him he jerked Robert back by the coat-tails. The fact that Cook was courting Robert's older sister saved Robert from anything worse.

School rivalry in those days was a serious matter; that between Cony and Gardiner high schools was very intense. I remember when we went to Gardiner for an away-from-home football game in the 1898 fall, that we were carefully warned to keep together in a tight Cony group, or we might get hurt.

On graduating from Cony High School in Augusta in 1902, I went to work for my uncle, Justin Penney (1858-1934), in Brockton, Massachusetts. He was a contracting carpenter employing about six men. He thought it was unusual for anyone to make much money working alone and that it was best to employ all the help that could be profitably used. I soon came to believe that he was right in this, and I have always tried to practice this lesson acquired so early in my life.

During the short time that I worked for my Uncle Justin, I was often employed as a helper for his best carpenter, George Engles. The first winter that I was on the job, early in 1903, we turned several hundred sign posts for the city of Brockton. This gave me good experience on the lathe, and I have always liked that tool to work with since.

Engles was a great joker. We were once working on the ground floor of a factory. When we had eaten dinner, George said to me, "Let's see what is doing upstairs." We found it to be a paper box factory, where 150 girls were having their nooning. They registered some interest when we entered the room, and they really brightened up when George said, "Here is a young fellow who wants to get married."

During this short interlude in my early life, I became well acquainted with my young cousin, Helen Penney (1892-19   ), Uncle

Justin's daughter. In 1914, she married Frederic Leon Hasey (1881-1949), and she became the mother of John Freeman Hasey (1916-), one of the outstanding young scions of the Penney family.

In 1904 thinking that the farm offered greater promise for me, I came back home.

Father came from a large family and had to pay the other members off with several thousand dollars. This was a large sum of money in the last century and for the first forty years in this one. Carrying this burden he had never been able to make the farm provide more than a bare living.

In 1907 my youngest brother, Justin (1888-1938) was provided with a farm at Belgrade Depot, but he was not successful and lost it.

There were one hundred acres of excellent land in the fields on the home farm, but Father had resorted to an exploitative system common in his day, keeping a small number of livestock and selling the surplus hay for the small but necessary income that it would bring. One distant field of nineteen acres had never been plowed in my memory. This field one year produced three loads of poor hay.

Harry and I worked together on the farm until 1911, when I decided to buy him out. Three appraisers set the amount due him at a few dollars less than three thousand dollars, which I was able to borrow.

On July 21, 1909, Miss Minnie Mills and I were married. At the time she said, "I hope we can take care of each other for a long time." It was the best thing that ever happened to me. She had such a cheerful and happy disposition that she seemed pleased, even with me.

We were able to move into a new house at the time of our marriage where we lived for our forty best years. Late in life after moving into another new house that we had built on the Penney farm some years ago, she said that it made her homesick to go back and visit our first home.

We had occasionally sold a little wood at the farm for four dollars a cord, cut, sawed, split and delivered. That looks like a low price from this distance in time, but in 1904 money was worth many times what it is now. In 1888 wood was furnished our school at three dollars a cord. Under date of 1836 wood was furnished the school at eighty cents per cord, and the teacher was boarded for one dollar and twelve cents per week. The winter ashes sold for thirty cents.

About 1910 I decided to sell stove wood in Augusta. I got up a considerable amount of wood and dried it under cover. I knew no one and I was very worried about finding a market for the first load. On the way to Augusta driving a team of horses with a sledload of wood, I met a neighbor, Ben Jellison, and he named three parties for me to contact. The first one took the wood and became a regular customer. I asked nine dollars a cord, delivered, but I later raised it to ten dollars. It cost a dollar or a little more to get it out, and it proved a profitable business.

With the purchase of our first farm truck in 1929, we sometimes could deliver two loads of stove wood per day and on rare occasions three.

There was a lot of softwood pulp on the Penney farm, and as soon as the bark could be peeled, we devoted all the time possible to harvesting at that season, as it brought more money and handled easily.

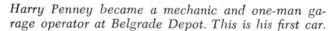

Harry Penney became a mechanic and one-man garage operator at Belgrade Depot. This is his first car.

During World War I, sugar was in very short supply. To compensate for this, I bought a hive of bees for ten dollars. It was some time before I learned to handle them. On one occasion they chased Minnie into the cellar. Our dog in the vicinity tried to get through the fence where he got stuck for a moment, most of the bees landing on him. Getting loose, he started down a steep grade at top speed. Here his legs went out from under him and he went end-over-end, losing most of the bees in the tumble. He finally found refuge in a hole at the house behind the door rock.

By purchase and swarming my bees increased to ten colonies. At the end of three years I had an extractor to separate the honey from the comb, quite a lot of other equipment, some experience, and they owed me one hundred dollars. From that point the business improved and during 1923 I sold $258.50 worth of honey.

Finally disease got into the hives and I had to close the interesting experiment with bees.

Mother raised turkeys for many years, and with Minnie's help, the flock sometimes numbered seventy-five. When small they are more delicate than common poultry. As soon as the fields are mowed they like to search there for grasshoppers and crickets. Walking abreast a foot or two apart, they would sweep the field. We were once threshing barley and some of the spills not being knocked off, the heads stuck in their throats giving them a lot of trouble. It was laughable to see the young turkeys fluttering on the ground scratching their necks first with one foot and then with the other.

One year our daughter, Dorothy, had a little bantam rooster, Peter, who was so tame that Dorothy could pick him up at any time. He decided that the big turkey gobbler had ruled long enough. He found that by grabbing the turkey by the head he could lead him around as long as he wanted to. When the gobbler would run away at the sight of the little giant, the bantam would crow exultingly. After having established his supremacy, the little bantam proudly led the flock of large birds in the fields.

The principal income in most of my time managing the Penney farm was from the dairy, and the livestock sold. 1904 is the first year of which I have a certain record. The returns that year from cream, cheese, and butter was $533.76. In 1907 it had risen to $700.00. In evaluating these figures it must be remembered that a dollar was worth much more at that time.

One fall we had a lot of birch bolts cut for the Oakland tooth-pick plant. Being out of material the company offered a premium of five dollars per cord for bolts delivered before a certain date. An unusual early snow allowed us to get the wood out easily and we shipped two carloads from Belgrade Depot in time to get the premium.

I found the improvement of pastures to be a very profitable enterprise on the farm. We had eighteen acres of land that had been annually pastured since it was cleared from woods, to the point where it produced very little grass. This caused the cattle to run in the woods where they should not be allowed, except in a small area for shade. I had Archie Bickford, a neighbor, plow this run-out area one fall. He was an expert teamster and he was able to strike out the lands as straight as a line could be drawn, although the plow was often out of the furrow between the cradle knolls. When the cattle were turned into the first crop of grass on this piece, the herd production was increased so noticeably that I received a prize from the Hood Company to whom I was selling milk.

When working a farm of this size over a period of many years, natural phenomena will sometimes be observed that the average country person may not see in a lifetime. There was a mirery place in the pasture that the cattle had to cross to reach the grass on the far side. I decided to make this crossing dry by laying logs for a corduroy. There were numerous trees handy for this purpose, many of them being dead ash with the loose bark hanging. When one of these was felled bats flew out. And while working on this job I found a small creature that I had never seen before, about two inches across, of a brown color, and rather inactive. It was a land crab. Very few farmers in this vicinity have ever seen one.

I always raised as much grain as possible. The straw chopped made excellent bedding, and the grain with supplement fed the cows. My records show that on April 30, 1946, 35 acres of oats were sowed on the farm. Mr. Bailey of the Central Maine Power Company saw my needs and when I was working in the back field

33

International Harvester
Titan 10-20 Tractor
1914—1924

The first Penney farm tractor; 1917

one day came and sold me a hammer mill of five horsepower and a grain mixer of 750 pounds capacity. The horses rested while this trade was made.

My generation in farming saw the evolution from the few and primitive farm machines used in the declining years of the last century to the many and very complicated labor-saving devices of the last decades. The machines that could be profitably used on a dairy farm I bought perhaps earlier than many other farmers in this region. I found that a farm could only survive through utilizing new ideas.

In 1917 I brought to the farm the first milking machine, an Empire model, and the first tractor, an International Harvester, to come into the town of Belgrade. And the Penney farm pioneered in many of the other mechanical conveniences over the nearly nine decades of my life.

When efficient field hay balers were first coming out right after the Second World War, Mr. Luce of the J. E. McCormick Company in Waterville reported that they could get only one. I gave him six hundred dollars immediately to bind that machine for the Penney farm. And I also bought a baled hay loader at the same time to ease and speed the work in the field. Angus McCormick, owner of this farm implement store, once helped me in 1926 to get a large thresher with blower attachment. This was a great help in our grain production. A few years later this was replaced with a combine, a machine that also threshed timothy whenever we needed seed. And in time we procured the hay baler with the automatic delivery of the bales to the hay wagon.

In 1938 the artificial breeding of cows was being talked about and practiced in some places. Mr. Norman Hamlin of Turner, milk tester in Kennebec County in 1939, went to New York to learn about the new method. When he returned to Maine, he came to see me, as I had an exceptional Jersey bull at that time that had increased my production by fifteen percent. He collected semen from this bull and bred three cows. One of these cows produced a calf, and it was exhibited with its artificially bred mother on a field day at the Monmouth State Experimental Farm. It was the principal attraction on that day, the first calf born in Maine from an artificially bred cow, sired by the Penney farm bull, Fairy Boy.

After 1950 we began to hear a lot about "tree farmers." I think I was one of the early ones. In 1926 we set out one thousand pine seedlings on the east side of the road. They have been thinned and pruned to the height of sixteen feet, and some of them are now one foot through on the stump. Several thousand pines have been set on the back of the farm, and these have also been pruned. When more essential work was not pressing, we would work on the pines. I have also sowed pine cones on many vacant areas. One year I planted a half bushel of white oak acorns, and they are doing well. All of a farm should be producing something.

In 1948 we built the small house that I now live in. In 1946 we bought and set up a sawmill on the farm. With this I was able to saw the lumber that had been cut on the farm—fifty thousand feet—for a new barn. When I finished building this barn, I was twelve thousand dollars in debt. The sawmill was a major element in getting this paid off at an early date.

For a long time we had needed a larger and better barn. In 1950 we decided to build a barn that would have every modern convenience then known and practical for this farm. We consulted an agricultural engineer, chose a site north of the old barn on a small ridge that had to be cut down nine feet for leveling, and had the foundation in by late in the fall. We cut and sawed the lumber in the 1950-51 winter, and the carpenters commenced to build early in the spring. Mr. Laurence Lyon was in charge of the five carpenters, and George and I and the hired men on the farm helped when we could.

We got the sides up and readily doubled-floored the hay loft. The roof was to be in a circle shape requiring the construction of laminated rafters built up from narrow boards in a form of this design on the floor. By the time we got to this phase, the hemlock boards had dried out so that they would not bend properly, so

The hog project on the farm, 1931.

36

they had to be put in the farm pond for a short period of soaking so that they would spring again. Finally sixty-two of these laminated rafters were assembled and all raised into place in the course of a single day. We then found that one recommendation of our engineer could not possibly be followed, that the roof boards be nailed on diagonally requiring springing the ends over a curve in the roof. Of necessity we nailed the roof boards horizontally.

During the course of our construction we discovered a shortage of two by twelve inch planks. Harry Knowles had some large hemlocks at the edge of my field! I paid him eighty-five dollars for what I needed and cut and sawed them out, giving us the needed planks with very little delay.

The new barn was completed in time to commence haying in June. It had four great conveniences that were thought quite wonderful at the time by the older generation of farmers, the hay conveyor, the gutter cleaner, the bulk tank, and a hopper to evenly distribute super phosphate on the manure as it left the barn at the push of a button. Farmers came from many miles around to see the new barn.

Two fans controlled by thermostats were installed insuring good ventilation, and a large manure shed was constructed with cement walls thirteen feet high.

While the manure shed was being built an agriculturist from a country in Europe called to observe the American system. He was much surprised to find me wheeling cement and rocks. He told me that in his country the owner didn't do such work, but simply gave instructions to others. I don't believe that he approved of me.

A hay dryer that we installed in the barn makes it possible to store hay before it is properly field dried in case rain threatens or for other causes. Hay comes out the very best from the dryer. I sold some that had been dried in this way to a lady, and she said it smelled so good that she planned to eat some of it herself.

The hay conditioner is another recent development in my life that compliments the older hay tedder in overcoming adverse weather.

All of these developments were quite beyond our dreams when I first went into the fields with Father in the 1890s.

Like all of the old Maine farms, tests showed that lime was very much needed on our fields by 1914. At first I had it come by railroad car, selling what I could to other farmers. After I had the first truck in 1929, I commenced to haul from Rockland directly. At first I bought the burned lime. I soon decided that the ground limestone was the best buy. One year I lacked only one load of putting on one hundred tons on the farm fields.

It is fifty miles to the lime plant in Rockland from the Penney farm, but I had a man working for me once who made three trips in one day. The fact that his girl friend was with him on this day may have made some difference. Love had come to them like a hurricane with thunder and lightning.

With only twenty-nine head of cattle of all ages, and two horses, I had to go out and buy hay the first year that I took over the farm and for several years after. As I soon increased the herd, I continued to have to buy hay. But in time my efforts paid off, and I got ahead of the animals and started selling hay every year.

At that time I was shipping cream, so there was a lot of skim milk for hogs available. I had an outdoor cooking kettle to boil five bushels of small potatoes in at one time. With the milk this made a very balanced ration. I remember how joyously the hogs would come tearing up to the troughs at feeding time. Perhaps they would have acted differently if they had known that I usually ate bacon for breakfast.

In 1903 we bought the first mechanical manure spreader to come into the town of Belgrade. It was called the Rock Island "Great Western," and with good care it lasted us for twenty years. When we finished with it, it was estimated to have spread over that long time six thousand loads. The record made by this spreader was brought to the attention of the manufacturer, and a picture of the relic was placed in their next sales catalogue.

Clarence Day, octogenarian historian of Maine agriculture, was county agent in Kennebec for a long time in the period of fifty years ago. He took a great interest in the Penney farm, brought material here for experiments to be performed under practical conditions, and in many other ways provided valuable information and assistance in the most fruitful years of my life.

There is reason to believe that many of the Penneys had aggressive traits somewhat above the average. When Nat Penney (1890-1934), Uncle Justin's son, was visiting her about 1894 at a very tender age, Grandmother tried to correct him. He bit and clawed his way out of her grasp in the process. She afterwards observed that never in her life had she been so ferociously attacked by such a small being.

These Penney traits have been especially conspicuous in one of our most outstanding scions, John Freeman Hasey (1916-   ), Uncle Justin's grandson and the son of my cousin, Helen Penney Hasey. John came to the farm a number of times to visit when he was a boy.

The onset of the Second World War in Europe found John Freeman working as a jewelry merchant in France. He went to Africa and the Middle East on campaign as an officer in the French Foreign Legion, and was badly wounded in Syria near Damascus. He came home recognized as the first American casualty in the Second World War.

Since the War he has had a fine career in our foreign service.

John Freeman Hasey, Lieutenant, French Foreign Legion, during the Second World War.

39

My greatest debt for whatever success I have had as a Maine farmer is to Minnie Mills Penney. This farm could not have prospered without her. On this large establishment there were often hired men as well as family to wash, cook, and mend for. Her health was never good, and a lesser woman would have given in to it. As it was she worked longer hours than I did. Many evenings she would be sewing, mending or canning. Hard work had been her lot since childhood. Work was the object in life, work was an end in itself in her code. Each year with much other work, she canned many hundreds of quarts of good food. If the raw materials fell off so that her production dropped a little in any year, this was an occasion for deep regret.

As I now look over her papers, I find that she kept an incredible number of records. The house I am living in, she inventoried when it was built with everything that went into it, down to the dustpan and broom. She seldom left the house or returned without setting down the exact times of departure and arrival.

In all of the local flower shows she usually took most of the first prizes. Many honors of more or less significance were granted to her in her lifetime by the Maine agricultural community and others. She earned all of them. She was an amateur student of birds and kept records of the varieties and their comings and goings.

All meetings of rural people are not without personal feelings and difficulties. Regardless of that, she always came back from her professional or social gatherings reporting to the stay-at-homes a good time.

As for me, a few years before he died, Father said, "You have done more to improve the place than anyone who has ever been on it."

HIRED MEN OF THE PENNEY FARM

Minnie made a list of the hired help we had to work on the farm after we were married. It was much larger than this. I have here enumerated those who labored here for such a period of time that they made a better-than-average contribution.

| Ray Nesbit | Chester Piper | Will Sawyer |
| Will Stevens | Clarence Fowler | Halton Grant |

The first spreader on our farm and the first one in Belgrade in
1903. Picture from the company sales catalogue of 1923.

Jean Winslow
Russell Sawyer
Earl Lovejoy
Cedric Young
Archie Bickford
Lloyd Cunningham
George Newell
Ted Newell
Lemond Dudley
Billy Burk
Harry Knowles
Frank Webb
Edward Gilby
Arthur Sylvester
Andrew Rowe
Lester Wyman
Guy Goodchilds
Guy Yeaton
Willie Mills
Felix Le Bounty
John de Aguier

Richard Fowler
Bill Scates
Buddy Knowles
George Dudley
Lloyd Harrison
Charles Webster
Clyde Batchelder
Charles Carl
Joe Kinney
Ed Knowles
Percy Chute
Harvey Smith
Joe Goodchilds
Clyde Varney
Harry Penney
Charles Mills
Nathan Bailey
Herman Hilton
Hanson Tufts
Wes Knowles
John Webster

Clyde Lyon
Lee Danforth
Jean Robinson
Leah Batchelder
Laura Fowler
Rose Mills
Oral & Connie Page
Abner & Bessie Dudley
Eban & Gertie Dudley
Harold & Laura Tripp
Clarence & Elizabeth
Jameson
Jean & Sarah Winslow
Elmer & Beverley
Kelley
Charles & Margaret
Thurston
John & Iva Richards
Floyd & Anna
Salsbury

41

Minnie Penney's Memories
of Her Early Life

I was born in Mapleton, Cumberland County, Nova Scotia, August 28, 1886.

There was a good deal of forest in our neighborhood and my father, Alexander Mills, did much lumbering in winter.

The maple syrup and sugar industry was also important in our area and many thousands of pounds were produced there, so that spring was an all-important time. We tapped well over two thousand trees. Maple products have a taste that is unique, and we were glad to entertain visitors and potential buyers to our farm. It took a lot of time to make the little birchbark containers for the candy, held together with wooden pins. Grated maple sugar was much used for sweetening in that place and time. The first of the run of sap made syrup that was almost transparent, and it was called the best.

Our school was nearly two miles away. There was no transportation and it was quite a walk for the little ones, especially in winter, when the roads were sometimes hardy passable for sleds. On the coldest days we would start well protected, with scarves and comforters and a hot potato in each hand.

There were five of us children in my family, and the nearby Bird family was even larger, so there wasn't much school until we arrived in a joint party.

In time we heard about automobiles, but we could hardly believe that there were such things, or that we would ever see one. But one day Father came running to the house shouting, "Come out, there is an automobile coming down Jim Bird's hill." No fire ever emptied a house so quickly, and there it was, laboring along slowly by modern standards. It was an "open" car. The women were wearing big hats with veils, and the men were clothed in "dusters" and long-wristed gloves. We were electrified when the travelers waved to us and blew their horn.

It was a race to school that morning to tell the great news, but we had to take second place, for one of the Bird boys stuck his thumbs under his suspenders and said, "You needn't feel so big about it. They stopped in our yard and changed a tire." That operation was a common thing in those days, and about the only sure place to get gasoline was in a drug store, where it was kept to clean gloves.

My mother, Lelia Augusta Gilroy (1864-1902), was always in poor health and, being the oldest, it fell to me to help out as soon as I could. Missing school in this way, I fell behind my class.

As soon as I could cook, a high box at the flour barrel enabled me to reach the mixing board. I made fast progress in home economics.

The Macon River was near, and the trout liked to lay in the shaded pools under the bridge, but they would usually refuse bait. But one day I landed one 17.5 inches long, the largest fish I ever caught. At another time I hooked an eel. Just as it happened, one of the Bird boys was coming by on his bicycle, and I jerked so violently on the line that the eel flew through the air and landed on his neck, throwing him off. He was very angry with me, thinking I had done it intentionally.

Spring Hill was six miles from our home, and Father having a large market garden, I often drove the horses to town, while he peddled vegetables at the houses.

We kept a number of horses, mostly to work in the woods during the winter, and in summer they ran in our pasture. To do an errand, it was sometimes necessary to catch one, and that was usually my job. I would take a halter and dish of grain and strike out, hoping to get the right one, which seldom happened. At sight of someone at the gate they would come tearing as if they were going to knock it down. It was some job to get the chosen one out, without the others bothering, ride him to the barn, and get ready to go.

With Mother's health so poorly, as far back as I can remember, I gladly took on more of the work in the house and the care of the younger children. I sometimes wondered if anyone was ever more tired. I worked away near the flour barrel standing on my box, and I seldom attended school. In spite of this the following is my report card for February, 1900:

Days present	6 out of 20 days school
Tardy marks	0
Reading	85
Spelling	90
Writing	100
Drawing	95
Composition	85
Health Reader	90
History	85
Arithmetic	87
Conduct	95

Signed: Georgia A. McKensey, teacher

Mother's death in 1902 ended my little schooling in the sixth grade.

It was allowed for one to commence teaching Sunday School at the age of fifteen. I was happy to start then and I have continued to teach for sixty-four years.

My classes have always been the little ones, many of whom have never been to school, and some without much, if any, discipline at home. The latter are often very difficult, presenting discouraging problems. But with patience on my part, they always improved and sometimes became models of deportment. I liked to teach Sunday School and I never thought of giving it up.

As I had gradually been taking over all of the house work, there was little change for me at the time of Mother's passing. We did have more hired men to care for about this time.

44

In 1903 Father married Rosanna Storey Smith (1874-1934) of South Brook. Her three children brought our five to eight, and I went to live with an aunt in Spring Hill and to learn dressmaking.

I had two aunts living on farms in Aroostook County, and Father visited them in 1905. He got the idea at this time of moving to Maine, but to locate there in the potato country would have required a lot of capital.

Father had a catalogue of farms for sale by the Strout Agency, represented in Augusta by W. D. Hutchins, reputed to be the first to own an automobile in that city. Father came to Augusta in due time. On leaving the train, he was approached by a driver of a canny nature, for he offered to take him to the Strout Agency for two dollars. It proved to be just across the square.

Mr. Hutchins showed Father the Scribner farm in West Sidney. It was a large farm with a good orchard, but situated on a side road. As the modern house afforded ample room for his large family, Father decided to make the purchase. He returned home to Nova Scotia to sell out. He found later that he was mistaken in thinking that the orchard in Sidney would equal the income derived from the maple grove in Nova Scotia.

The next thing was an auction, a sad occasion in parting with so many things that had been with us for so long. This auction brought in over three thousand dollars, which Father thought was very satisfactory.

We had never traveled very much from home, and it seemed a strange and fearsome thing to leave the old farm and pioneer in a new country. The only livestock we took with us was our faithful dog, Danger, and he was really one of the family.

Our arrival in West Sidney was anticipated, and the piazza at our next door neighbor's house was crowded with people gathered to appraise the new comers. It was July 26, 1906. One of our new friends conveyed us from Belgrade Depot to the farm in a hayrack, as he had been told there would be many trunks. We must have looked like a band of gipsies.

Soon we all came down with homesickness, especially Danger. If anyone started for the road, he would run on ahead in the vain hope that we were starting back for Nova Scotia. He moped for days and would not eat.

Our nearest neighbor was the Sunday School superintendent, and I took my quarterly from back home to see if she used the same one. She gave me a class of boys for the following Sunday, so the shift in my Sunday School teaching was made without a break.

Her father, Mr. Lovejoy, was messenger of the State Senate for many years, and well acquainted in Augusta. He soon got me a job as a domestic in the family of one of his relatives. As I came home on Saturdays for the weekend, I still continued with my Sunday School.

When the Legislature was in session, Mr. Lovejoy took me to church every Sunday, and he was so well acquainted, and introduced me to so many people, that it was a pleasure to go with him. I soon had a close friend in a nice girl, and we were together when possible, until she found that I was a domestic worker. Then she wouldn't notice me at all. This all seemed very strange to me at the time, but it may have been common. Her father was State Librarian.

After about a year, I was loaned by the family I worked for to a family of their relatives, who were expecting. There were two families in a large house with more idea of class than money, as I often heard of their bank account being overdrawn. The wife of the elder couple ruled the entire domain, at least in the house.

The younger couple had a boy, almost of school age, who had never been house broken. One of my jobs was to clean him up and often. Mrs. Fuller would lead him out and say, " He has had an accident." One day when I had cleaned him up, and the folks were away, I gave him such a spanking as he had never known. I told him that if he made any more trouble, he would get twice as much. Mrs. Fuller soon inquired about what had happened to change him so completely.

One day when I was home in West Sidney in 1908, Miss Lovejoy, the Sunday School superintendent, and I visited the Penney farm in Belgrade. This was when I first met Willie (I always called him that), my future husband. We afterwards met in

46

Grange, and I became a close friend of his sister, Jessie, and visited her on the Penney farm when possible.

There was an Augusta excursion boat at that time that made daily trips in season to the islands at the mouth of the Kennebec River, and Willie and I took one of these trips. On the way home he asked me to marry him. As he planned to build a house before we were married, we could not set a date. I kept on working.

An old house stood on the Penney place, past repair, and Willie took this down for the brick and underpinning which was found in great abundance. A cellar was dug and the foundation placed for the new house in the fall of 1908. The lumber was gotten out and sawed that winter, and construction work commenced in the spring of 1909, with three carpenters at $2.50 per day each. Willie hired a replacement on the farm, so that he could give his time to the house.

We were married on July 21, 1909, and moved into the new house the next day. Construction costs were much different then, as may be seen by the comparative daily cost of carpenters. One thousand board feet of maple flooring was bought out of the railroad car for fifty dollars to be used in our home.

Although the prices of material seem very low compared with those of later years, we still had to practice strict economy. I used to say, " I will buy only what farmers can afford." We never forgot then that we were very poor.

The old fashioned way of rolling down new fallen snow on the road by the Penney farm. That continued until about 1928.

47

Willie's brother was the other heir to the Penney farm, and we decided to buy him out. The appraisers set Harry's share at just under three thousand dollars and we were able to borrow that. We got off to rather a slow start, as the farm was not producing feed sufficient for twenty-nine cattle and two horses, and it was necessary to buy for several years.

Willie went to raising potatoes, and one of our first crops was very bountiful on a large acreage for these parts. We received ninety-seven cents a bushel. We were not quite that lucky again, and one year we sold at ten cents a bushel.

From the first of our marriage Willie commenced to cut wood to sell. It was the best hard wood and dried under cover, and one day in the fall, Willie started to Augusta with his first load, not knowing where it would go. On the way he met a neighbor, who told him of a good prospect who, as it happened, was glad to buy. This was our start in what proved to be for us a very good business selling stove wood.

Sometimes wood delivery wasn't easy, especially when the roads were not broken, and there was an urgent call from someone who was cold. Once Willie started with the team and the load on a winter day. It started to snow hard and it was impossible to keep to the road and he had to take to the fields adjoining. On arriving in Augusta, the horses were so hot and exhausted that he bought a box of ginger and mixed it in their grain to prevent them from catching cold.

At another time there was plenty of snow for good sledding, but the Augusta bridge was bare, and there we got stuck blocking traffic. The horses had never known anything like that, but they did their best, one shedding two shoes, which a bystander handed to me, as a crowd had gathered. But somebody called the police, and they came with a big truck and pushed us across. The two shoes were tacked on at a blacksmith shop where the Cottle Market parking lot now stands.

The price for stove wood when we started in the business was nine dollars per cord, sawed, split, dried and delivered. Money was worth several times what it is now. Willie sold many hundreds of cords to various parties and not more than four failed to pay. One party that we supplied for many years had to have the wood carried up stairs, but we made no extra charge.

When Willie got to hauling wood with a truck about 1929, he lost his tailboard with considerable wood when going through French Town in Augusta on one trip. He went right back as soon as he discovered what had happened, but the street had been cleaned and swept of stove wood.

Willie always shoed his own horses, unless there was a new one that had never been shod. It is a pretty bad horse that won't stand to be shoed.

We had a great abundance of wood on the Penney farm, and perhaps we were fortunate to dispose of as much as we did before people turned to oil heating in the 1930s and 1940s. Our biggest mistake in getting out wood was to put birdseye maple logs into stove wood.

Sometimes when a tree was lodged, Willie would go up to top off some limbs to let it down, a very dangerous job. Once a helper, when Willie was about to start this operation, asked, "Have you any message you would like to leave?"

One day at noon about the last of March, 1912, Willie said to me, "Don't you want to go over to your Father's this afternoon and get that calf he has for me?" And I said, " I'd be delighted to." It was a warm, spring day. Old Sandy, the horse we used for driving, was afraid of automobiles. As the mud was so deep and it was so early in the spring, I didn't think any of them would be on the road yet. Old Sandy was usually a good old horse, and I thought I could manage him easily, with baby Dorothy in my arms and the reins in my hands.

Everything went well going over, and I got the calf in a grain bag, with his head sticking out, under the wagon seat. Mother Mills gave me a rooster in another bag, which I put down at my feet. Dorothy was asleep when I took her in my arms and started on the two and a half miles home. I got about half way, when I saw an automobile coming. Sandy saw it at the same time and began to prance. I tried to talk to him and calm him down, but it was no use. He stood right on his hind legs and pawed the air. As the auto neared, I stuck out my hand for the occupants to stop.

Two men got out very hurriedly and came running up and pulled Sandy down out of the air, getting all four feet securely on the ground. One of the men said, " He's pretty scared, ain't he? " I said, "So am I. I have a baby in my arms, a calf under the seat, a rooster at my feet, and I sure don't want to get dumped." I braced myself, got a good grip on the reins, and we sailed off, leaving the two men standing and laughing in the road.

About ten years later Dorothy had another dangerous experience with a horse. She was sitting in Bert Farnham's (1880-1949) wagon at Belgrade Depot with young Frank Farnham, then a small child. Bert had gone into a store, leaving the horse unhitched. The railroad passes through town at that point, and a train started coming by. This frightened the horse, and he started to run very fast and right towards the train. Dorothy grabbed Frank and sprang out of the wagon. The horse ran against the train and fell under it, and the wheels passed over his head.

Upon arrival home, Dorothy did not report the exciting event. We found out about it the next day, when Frank's mother called to thank Dorothy for saving his life. Upon being asked why she had not told us, she said, "I didn't think it was very important. Nobody got hurt."

We soon found out that securing enough help on our farm was one of our problems. We tried to get the work done at the proper time for the best returns with hired help, when that was possible. I have known what it meant to wash, cook, and mend for several hired men all of my life. Our first hired man, or rather boy, was Ray Nesbit, and he was good. Our hired men liked to go fishing and they often went to Penney Pond in the evenings. Here they would build a fire on the shore and pull in the fish, mostly horned pout. The best night I remember they caught two hundred and twelve. Two hooks on each line would have fish.

The family in 1915: Will, Dorothy and Minnie Penney.

In July, 1924, I was elécted president and Mabel Farnham vice president of our Belgrade Ladies' Aid, taking the places of Lillian Yeaton and Cora Penney. We realized that we had a heavy load on our shoulders, but we were quite young and venturesome. We were both on the same telephone line and we kept it busy with many long conversations in regards to our new positions.

We went to work and, with the support of all the members, commenced talking about the building of a steeple on the church at Rockwood's Corner and securing a bell for it. When the men saw that we were really earnest, they came to the front with generous contributions. In 1925 the steeple and bell were installed.

This success gave us more courage, so in that same year we had the church painted, electric lights and lightning rods added, and a weather vane placed on the steeple, the last the gift of George Weaver.

In 1928 Blanche Minot, my close friend, donated cushions for every seat in the church. I don't think anyone who knows can ever look at them without thinking of our dear Blanche and of the many other nice things she did for us.

Winter was a busy time on our farm. There was the ice to cut, haul from the stream, and store for the milk tank in the summer.

An outcrop of ledge on the road to Belgrade stream proved to be a bad obstacle during the ice harvest, and Willie decided to blow it out. He drilled thirty inches into the ledge and put in two sticks of dynamite with a fuse and lit it, but it failed to fire. After about fifteen minutes he cut the fuse off at the ledge and relit it. After another wait of about fifteen minutes, he had picked up a spoon a short distance away to dig out the stemming to put in a new stick on top, when it fired. This was another one of numerous narrow escapes that happened to us.

At another time Willie was knocked down by a big bull on our farm that held him to the ground, but he got hold of the ring in the bull's nose and wound it until the bull drew back, giving him a chance to scale a nearby fence.

I have always taken care of the hens on our farm. I commenced with a flock at the start of our married life, and for a long time I raised my own chickens from the eggs. This was my own principal income, and from this I often bought necessary things for the home. My flock usually numbered around one hundred birds. In one egg-laying contest of ten leading flocks, mine came out first with 22.6 eggs per bird in one month of October.

52

Jersey calves in the farm barn.

As the condition of the farm improved, there was hay to sell, and on two occasions large stacks had to be made in the field, as there was not sufficient barn space. Although the livestock had more than doubled from our beginnings, in 1919 we sold hay to the amount of $716.87. That was the big year, but we continued to sell after the herd had passed one hundred head.

Minnie Penney's Diary: 1926-1967

In 1926 I commenced keeping a diary. It was almost always written in bed, after the day's work, and I continued with it for more than forty years.

[The following is only a small fraction of the entries from a very voluminous record of life in the Penney Farm. Entries are left as they appeared in the diary.]

1926

FEBRUARY 28. Willie went to Waterville to see about electric lights. Not much encouragement.

MARCH 10. First crow put in appearance.

MARCH 15. Red polls and chickerdees.

APRIL 12. Robins.

Minnie Mills Penney with one of the turkeys about 1917.

54

APRIL 26. Had a pine tree planting demonstration here to-day. Set three hens. Made an apron and two bureau scarves. Got auto licenses. First frogs.

APRIL 22. First wild geese — three flocks.

APRIL 24. Swallows came, and four bald eagles flew over.

MAY 25. Mother and I took eight bushels of danderlion greens to Augusta. Got $8.25 for them. Turned cows out for first time.

JUNE 22. We went to the "Willows" to hear Mellie Dunham play. It was grand. 2000 or more cars with 5000 or more people.

AUGUST 18. Willie went to Waterville for new threshing machine. I carried cream, and went to Ladies' Aid in afternoon.

AUGUST 20. Canned 18 quarts of beans, 4 quarts peas, 4 quarts sweet mixed pickles, and put up 85 quarts of honey.

1927

JANUARY 12. Mother, Willie and I went to Farm Bureau planning meeting. A nice time. I am clothing project leader for 1927.

FEBRUARY 19. Stormy. They plowed the road from Sidney Corner to Belgrade Lakes. Ten horses and 14 men.

AUGUST 23. Willie and I went to Augusta. I washed and ironed. Etta Lovejoy passed away. We owe her a big debt as she introduced us.

Dolly & Jack 1932

Cultivating corn 1932

SEPTEMBER 20. They came with new Maytag washer, and did our washing.

OCTOBER 3. I washed with my new machine, and made three kinds of pickles.

OCTOBER 9. We went over home for family reunion. There were 32 present.

We bought our first car in 1927, and I drove it from the first, maybe more than anyone else. It was a great pleasure and convenience.

1933

FEBRUARY 24. Willie still sick. Dr. Stubbs said, " Rest ten days more."

MARCH 24. Willie is up, feeling better. I did my ironing.

MARCH 30. Went to Augusta with Willie. X-ray shows his lungs have not cleared up, so he has to go back to bed.

APRIL 10. Dr. says Willie must not work for a month.

MAY 11. Made two dresses today, one for Mrs. Pressey, and one for myself.

JUNE 22. Dance hall opened. The Willows.

OCTOBER 13. Had my tonsils out. Dr. Fallon did the job. Home in bed at 2:30 p.m.

OCTOBER 15. Oh, what a sore throat!

OCTOBER 16. Throat better. Did some mending. Made cake.

One of the more interesting things that happened to me in this 1933 year, was the giving of a radio talk on Sewing With Your Daughter for the University of Maine Extension Service. This was broadcast over several Maine radio stations on July 27, 1933. As it relates something of my life on the farm at that time, I include it as follows:

" With the women who have daughters of any size or age, I'd like to have a friendly talk this morning on the subject of making your own clothes. ' What about those who have sons to outfit?' you ask. After the age of seven or eight their suits must come chiefly from the store ready-made. The mothers and daughters sew at any time.

" My first experience with a needle came as a little girl, when a dressmaker next door began supplying me with pieces of cloth for dolls' dresses. She also gave me instructions about cutting, fitting, stitching, and pressing. A few pieces later, I found myself elected the family dressmaker, as well as instructor and assistant to my mother and five sisters.

"Not only then but ever since this experience has proven a valuable asset to me. The biggest and most recent project has been to clothe a daughter in high school and college. I should say help clothe as I had reintroduced the happy lessons of the doll clothes, and with the aid of the sewing project in the local 4-H club, my daughter soon learned the new and more up-to-date methods, and we have sewed together for the last five years.

"Girls are especially conscious of their clothes during their high school and college years. Mothers must be both sympathetic onlookers and helpful assistants when the young enthusiasts bring home ten or fourteen piece patterns for fitting suits, party, and evening dresses.

"By making our own clothes, we can more easily have the pattern style we want combined with the desired material and color. Often two or three old patterns can be remodeled with little care into individually distinctive and desirable lines.

"Then comes the question of remodeling old garments. When I answered the doorbell the other day, a charity worker asked me, 'Have you any particular use for old clothes?' Perhaps I answered a little selfishly, but I said, 'You bet I have; I wear them myself.'

"In my particular case, my daughter has been, and still is, somewhat slimmer than I am and wears her dresses shorter, too. A dress of mine, which was perfectly good, was cut down for her and fitted up with new collar and cuffs. In this way a new dress has been added to her wardrobe. A last summer's navy blue coat made an appropriate jumper dress for her. Of course many of you have seen pictures of the surprising results obtained by adding new yolk tops to dresses, boleros, bows, sleeves, and collars and cuffs.

"A school vacation always means to my daughter and me a going-over of our two wardrobes to retouch and remodel. By making our own and our daughter's dresses, we can save money, and yet have just as good, if not better, material and resulting effects. Recently a friend of mine said that her daughter, who is in the first year of high school, told her that she liked the dresses made at home better than the cheap, ready-made ones.

"They are nicer and prettier. It is a real saving in cash to do home sewing. This year my daughter and I saved on an average of fifteen dollars a month by doing just this. For instance, we found that an evening wrap of black chiffon velvet cost $4.50 to make, while one in the store window like it was marked $9.98. A two-tone party dress, in just the color and style desired, cost $6.50 less than its store sister.

"Money saved from making our own clothes, when combined with the proceeds from chicken-raising, and that saved from the grocery allotment by canning around 550 quarts of garden products each year, helped me to equip my home with modern conveniences and labor-saving devices. Thrift in one line helps to start and increase thrift in others. I say that it pays for mothers to sew for and with their daughters, and if you will keep a budget of expenses and approximate money saved, you will be surprised and pleased with the results."

The last load of hay going to the barn in 1932 on July 25.

1934

JANUARY 8. George and I some better, but Willie is sick, telephone line broken, wind won't blow to pump water. Boys having hard time.

JANUARY 12. Willie and I went to Farm Bureau, election of officers. I am president and 4-H leader.

.... Tacking quilt all my spare time. When Jill Gregoire came in, puffing a cigarette, I asked him to help tack the puff. He said, "I had rather puff this tack."

FEBRUARY 26. Mother Mills taken sick this forenoon, but better at night.

.... She passed away at 3 A.M. Willie, my brother, came for me, and I helped lay her out.

MARCH 5. Ironed and went to high school time. Was sick and had doctor.

1935

JANUARY 2. No school, no mail. The most terrible storm in a great many years. Twelve school children had to spend the night at a neighbor's house. Four car loads of men were stalled at another place over night.

JANUARY 8. Willie had a letter from Merton Knowles stating that he could have the Manley Knowles place for $400. The asking price was $800. It is about 40 acres and very well situated for us. It was once the home of Elias Taylor, Willie's grandfather's great-grandfather, who was the first white child born in Augusta, 1762.

JANUARY 18. Elected Farm Bureau officers for year. I was chosen 4-H club leader.

JANUARY 19. A tramp came. I gave him dinner, and kept him all night.

JANUARY 28. Monday. Awful storm. Got our mail. First delivery since Wednesday.

FEBRUARY 2. Saturday. We have had a 4-H club meeting. 20 members present.

FEBRUARY 16. Another club meeting. 20 present, a nice time.

MARCH 12. Have made 30 lbs. hard soap and used up all my grease.

MARCH 13. Willie gave talk over radio today.

MARCH 14. Had a letter from Helen Spaulding asking me to make a speech at Orono, March 25.

.... Started for Orono. Went up to the Depot on school bus, then on train. Had dinner in Bangor, then to Orono on trolley. Attended many interesting meetings and saw the outstanding homemakers and farmers honored.

MARCH 27. Went to clothing leaders convention. Had a very fine program. Went to the banquet, over 1000 seated. We started for our room with newspaper over our heads, it was snowing so hard.

MARCH 29. Came home from Orono.

APRIL 17. Sick and not able to go to Executive meeting.

APRIL 20. I went to Grange alone, Old Maids' Convention, very fine.

APRIL 27. Went to 4-H club conference. 33 present, had a delightful time.

APRIL 28. Went to see Blanche Minot, who is very ill. Took her nice white linen fur pillow, some parsnips and dandelion greens, and some Mayflowers. She gave me another of her pictures, making six that we have. She is an art teacher, and her pictures are very good. I have taken her on many trips in the car, and she is a very dear friend.

MAY 5. Sunday School started. 50 present. I had 14 in my class.

1937
MARCH 22. Started for Orono at 9:30, had a nice trip up on train. When I arrived in Bangor, Mr. Clarence Day and Mr. Conant met me, and we had dinner in town. I was given room No. 1 on the first floor when I arrived at the University, with Mrs. Hoyt for a roommate.

The Penney farm as it appeared in 1934.

MARCH 25. I had to sit at the head table with President Arthur Hauck tonight, then went on stage with 17 others and took part in receiving the State of Maine Banner.

When conferring the honor of Chief Homemaker on me, President Hauck spoke as follows:

"You have proven your ability as a housekeeper and homemaker, both in your father's home, when scarcely more than a child, as the head of a motherless household, and in your own home on one of the largest dairy farms in Kennebec County, where hired help is constantly employed.

"But your interests have reached beyond the pleasant home which you and your husband have made, and you have been a tower of strength in the community. You have been active in the church, having taught a class in Sunday School since you were fifteen, and have served as President of the Ladies' Aid for many years. In the Grange you have held various offices, having served on the executive committee for fourteen years. You have been especially active in encouraging adult education through the

Farm Bureau, and in giving the young people of Belgrade a broader training and vision through the 4-H club of which you have been the local leader for several years. For seven years you were a member of the executive committee of the Kennebec Farm Bureau.

"It is a pleasure for the University of Maine to honor you as an outstanding homemaker."

MARCH 26. Came home from the University of Maine with Miss Katherine Potter, Mr. Blackstone from Caribou, and Mrs. Milton Smiley of Winslow.

1938

JANUARY 15. Harvey came over at eight o'clock, as Papa had passed away. I stayed until noon, then came home. Then at one o'clock Charlie Mills called for me to go to Augusta with him and Willie to get casket and flowers. Then Willie brought me home at six.

JANUARY 17. Willie, George, and I went to Papa's funeral. Large number present. Rose and Winfield came from Massachusetts. All the family were present.

JANUARY 22. Had a mean day. Did too much walking yesterday. Finished getting ice. Six men to dinner. Willie took a load of wood to Augusta, and then on to Bowdoinham for fertilizer.

JANUARY 24. Willie went on conservation work. He then took load of wood to Augusta and brought back load of grain.

JANUARY 28. I made 10 pies today, 7 pumpkin, two apple, and one lemon.

JANUARY 31. No water, so I couldn't wash, so I mended clothes all day.

FEBRUARY 3. Willie went to Augusta in A.M. Got conservation check, $158.60.

FEBRUARY 5. Did general Saturday work in A.M. Had 4-H down here, nice time. Made muffins and ate them. Had candy and popcorn. I took them home.

FEBRUARY 10. Made 20 quarts of mince meat, and two big dishes of hogshead cheese. Milk tester came. Willie finished conservation work in Rome.

FEBRUARY 11. I made 11 pies today, have put beans in oven, and made yeast bread, and also mended some.

FEBRUARY 25. Had 4-H club meeting at school house. 9 present. Finished yellow dress. That makes three I have made this week.

MARCH 1. I made donuts. Finished another dress. Lost cow with lockjaw.

MARCH 5. Stayed in bed all day. Had Dr. McKay at noon. He said I had bronchitis and laryngitis, and to stay in bed.

MARCH 6. Terrible week. Have lost 7 pounds.

MARCH 8. Grandpa came from Portland. I didn't do much but cook and mend stockings. Grandpa had supper with us, and stayed all night.

MARCH 28. Did not wash. Water was scarce. Made 18 lbs. more hard soap. That is 42 lbs. in all. Set one hen on 15 eggs.

APRIL 5. Just fussed around and cooked for six men. Snow gone from lane.

APRIL 12. Cooked out lard and cared for all the fresh pork.

APRIL 14. I spaded my flower bed. Bill was burning brush and it got away. We helped him put it out.

APRIL 16. Got up early and got ready and took Hattie Sheaff and went to Manchester to 4-H club leaders' conference. Had a fine time.

APRIL 23. Went to 4-H club at Sheaff's. Had a nice time. The wildcat came last night and gave us a good serenade.

APRIL 25. Did a very large washing, three heavy quilts, seven rugs, five blankets, and a lot of overalls and frocks. Cleaned one room.

MAY 5. Harold Chaput went three trips to Rockland for land lime.

MAY 7. At 9:30 A.M. twelve of my club members came. They cooked the dinner, and dug 20 pecks of danderlion greens, and sold them at .25 cents a peck. $5.00.

MAY 8. A female prometheus moth hatched out of the cocoon we got on a cherry tree in the winter. Very lovely.

MAY 12. Male prometheus moth hatched out. Went to Farm Bureau meeting at Mrs. Sheaff's. Took my butterflies.

Rockwood Meeting House in Belgrade where Minnie Penney taught Sunday School for many years.

May 14. Hustled and got ready to go to the State Dress Review. Took Mrs. Lyon and Hattie Sheaff. Hattie got third. Had a nice time.

May 18. Papered some more. Canned 9 pints of pea soup and 6 pints of danderlions. Made head cheese. Cooked out lard. Transplanted some petunias.

May 25. Got 4 nice blue spruce, and Willie and I set them out. We also got a lot of other little trees to set out, spruce, fir, cedar, pine, Norway pine, and hemlock. 33 in all set out now. Very pretty.

May 29. I went to church and Sunday School. Mrs. Lyon and I went to cemetery with flowers. The lots look fine.

June 13. Washed. Went to see Dr. McKay. He said my blood pressure is too high.

June 19. Did not feel able to go to church.

June 20. Started haying.

June 22. Willie and I went to Augusta. Dr. McKay found my blood pressure normal. Jean Robinson came to work for me. She is good help.

June 25. Had 4-H club meeting on Leah Bachelder's lawn. There were nine members present, four visitors and one leader. Plans were made for the county field day next week at the Music Camp.

July 8. Grammie Penney fell and broke her shoulder one year ago today.

July 21. The army worms came in full force and destroyed our grain.

July 26. Willie and I went to Augusta this A.M., where I got the judges for the flower show.

July 28. Lots of flowers at the show. I got first, second, and third prizes.

August 1. Washed. Had Laura Tripp and the kiddies over to supper. Cut Laura's hair. Miss Childs came and brought Clayton Huntley to help us.

August 12. Went picking blueberries and blackberries. Made 48 blueberry muffins for supper.

August 13. Cooked all A.M. Went to 4-H club meeting.

August 14. Clayton and I went to church and Sunday School, then hurried home, ate dinner, then took Mrs. Lyon and went to Manchester to hear Wallace Nutting preach.* The church was packed. We got his autobiography.

August 16. George and Clayton took the truck and went to the Depot for the 4-H kiddies. We had a picnic at Summer Haven. It was very, very hot.

August 17. Mrs. Lyon, Grandpa, Jean and I went over to Jacques Turkey Ranch.

August 25. Jean and I canned 22 quarts string beans. Finished haying.

August 26. Threshed today. Harold Sheaff and Walter Buker helped our five men. Ate first melon today, got two nice ones. We have a picture of one weighing 13½ lbs.

August 28. Got three nice melons. My birthday. Got a lot of nice presents.

August 31. Ladies' Aid met with Donna Yeaton. Good crowd and a nice time in her lovely new house. Jean was away to her family reunion.

September 10. Have had 11 to dinner for three days. Threshing and picking corn.

.... Worked hard all A.M. getting ready for company. Sister Bessie and Mary Cushman came and spent the afternoon. After they went, I went to Nina Page's and Ed Cottle's wedding, then to the hall for a big reception.

September 18. George and Grandpa started for Aroostook at 6:45 A.M.

September 24. Jean and I canned today. String beans 1, rhubarb 6, shell beans 3, beets 17, jam 2, jelly 8. This P.M. went to Winthrop and got 7 bushels of apples.

September 30. Friday. Had a crowd filling 3rd silo. 9 in all. Corn all in.

October 8. Did general house work and cooked. Had crowd threshing beans. Have 460 quarts canned and 115 glasses of jelly.

*The famous antiquarian who had lived in that neighborhood as a boy.

OCTOBER 13. Made a dress for myself, real pleased with it, rust color rayon print.

OCTOBER 19. The sad news of the death of Justin Penney, Willie's brother, came today.

OCTOBER 21. Very sad day. Justin's funeral was a large one. We had 15 to dinner.

OCTOBER 27. George, Eben Lord and I started for Massachusetts at 7:00 A.M. Had a nice trip and arrived at 32 Lawrence St., Danvers at 2:00 P.M. They took me to Needham to my sister's and the rest all went back.

OCTOBER 29. I sewed for Rose all A.M. while she cooked, and in the P.M. we went shopping. To movies in the evening.

NOVEMBER 2. Sewed and cooked. In P.M. Jean and I went to Augusta to see Dr. McKay. He said I had arthritis in my knee. Had club meeting after school.

NOVEMBER 5. Jean and I took seven 4-H club members to the county contest at Cony High School in Augusta. Had a fine but tiresome time. Jean went home.

NOVEMBER 8. Went to Ladies' Aid Fair. Good crowd. We cleared $137.66.

NOVEMBER 13. I did not go to church. My knee was too bad.

NOVEMBER 19. Made 6 pies. Willie extracted honey. Canned 4 quarts baked beans.

NOVEMBER 22. Went to Mt. Vernon to see Dr. Moore. He said rheumatic arthritis caused by fallen arches and overweight, so put me on strict diet. Blood 200.

NOVEMBER 25. Started snowing and blowing in the night and very much colder. A terrible day, snowing and big drifts. No mail. Grandpa stayed.

NOVEMBER 30. This P.M. Jean and I went to Mt. Vernon to see Dr. Moore. He found me better. My blood pressure had gone down from 200 to 160. Good.

.... Sewing for 1938: 8 dresses, 5 aprons, 5 slips, 10 pillow slips, 20 sugar bags made into various articles, 6 holders, 6 dresses for baby.

JANUARY 1. Everyone away. Willie and I have been alone all day.

JANUARY 4. I just fussed around all day. Didn't do enough to notice.

JANUARY 8. Everett took a load of wood to the Gregoires and tipped the truck over in their yard, but no harm done that can be seen.

JANUARY 9. Washed, ironed and mended. I am real tired tonight. The men started setting the electric light poles. A Sears order came today. Everything O.K.

JANUARY 18. Cleaned up the house and got ready for company. Harry Bickford called to see about electricity. George and Everett caught a red fox in trap.

JANUARY 26. The boys sold their 4 fox skins for $18. George took a load of popple to Oakland. Willie took 50 bushels of beans to Monmouth and got $96.85.

FEBRUARY 25. Cleaned the cellar. Made an apron. Knitted a lot. Willie took a load of wood and onions to the county jail, and got a load of grain.

MARCH 8. The electric refrigerator and washing machine came today.

MARCH 13. Grandpa came home from Portland. A very stormy day. The men picked over beans. The Augusta mail came but none from Belgrade. No school.

MARCH 17. The roads were broken about 3:00 P.M. There were 15 men to shovel.

MARCH 27. Willie and I started at 8:30 for Orono to attend Farmers' Week at the University of Maine. Have a room at Clarence Day's. Met lots of old friends. Mahlon Knight of Kennebec County was honored as an outstanding farmer.

APRIL 16. Got up early and went for a walk before breakfast. Did up work and went out to walk again. Lovely spring morning. Willie and I are alone.

APRIL 23. Took off all blankets and put sheets on beds. Andrew Rowe came to work.

APRIL 28. Finished my blue and white dress, and cut out flowery percale dress. Willie went to Skowhegan and bought two horses, "Jim" and "Sandy". Grandpa is still in bed.

APRIL 29. Grandpa not so well. We had Dr. Moore. He says Grandpa is threatened with pneumonia. Willie went to Augusta to get some medicine. Dr. Moore came again tonight and found Grandpa slightly better.

MAY 10. Grandpa is very low. Dr. says he may last a week.

MAY 13. No new developments in Grandpa's case, only weaker and loss of speech at night. Grandpa passed away at 11:10 P.M.

MAY 14. Willie and I went to Augusta and picked out a casket and sent telegrams, then went to see the sexton.

MAY 16. A sad day. Grandpa's funeral. A lot of folks came.

MAY 18. Electricity was turned on for first time at 2:15 P.M. Great rejoicing.

MAY 21. Sunday. Willie set out oak trees beside the road.

MAY 22. We washed with the new electric washer this A.M. and went to Augusta.

J. Newton Penney (1852-1939) working with his oxen on the Penney farm about 1900.

JUNE 9. Did housework and cut out a dress in A.M. Finished dress in P.M. and wore it to grammar school graduation. Once at suppertime I showed the boys a piece of cloth, and told them I would be wearing it at breakfast time, and I did.

JUNE 18. Went to church and Sunday School. Chickens crowded and 37 died. Tough luck.

JUNE 21. A new man, Mr. Alton Richardson came, and we hired another, Felix Le Bounty. The last was a good man and stayed a long time.

JULY 6. Canned 22 quarts of strawberries. The New England Telephone Co. staked out the line today.

JULY 17. I didn't wash. No water, but mended a lot.

JULY 18. Two Central Maine Power Co. men came and figured on new water system.

JULY 21. Dot and Ken sent us an electric fan for our 30th wedding anniversary present. Jean made us a nice anniversary cake.

JULY 30. Sunday. We put in a telephone at barn.

AUGUST 5. The men have been digging holes and set the telephone poles today.

AUGUST 13. Sunday. Willie and I went to Manchester Church to hear Wallace Nutting. There was a very large crowd out.

AUGUST 14. We all went down to Manchester to hear Wallace Nutting give an illustrated lecture. Very fine.

AUGUST 15. We went to a picnic at Endicott's grove. The men had bad luck at the threshing. The tractor caught fire and, as it was covered with oil, it blazed up like a brush pile. It was a very dangerous place for a fire. Willie threw it into reverse, breaking the belt, and backed it into the barnyard. His hands were burned. By throwing dirt on the engine, the fire was soon put out. Had to replace wires.

AUGUST 20. Felix Le Bounty, Mary Niles, Willie and I started at 8:30 A.M. for the White Mountains. Had a wonderful trip through New Hampshire and part of Vermont. Came home through Crawford Notch, supper at Jessie's home at 8:30 P.M. Trip was 349 miles. Felix had lived there, so he was a good guide.

AUGUST 25.   The men finished threshing over 1000 bushels of oats. Got stung by a bee. No fun.

AUGUST 28.   Jessie, Arlene and I started for Bar Harbor to see Dot and Ken.

SEPTEMBER 3.   Went to Sunday School and church. The war news is awful bad. England and France have declared war.

SEPTEMBER 12.   The New England Telephone Co. is putting up the wire today.

SEPTEMBER 24.   Went to Sunday School and church. Then Willie and I went for a ride over on the Dunn road where the Penneys lived on first coming to Belgrade.

SEPTEMBER 29.   A well driller came and got the job.

OCTOBER 18.   Well drilling stopped for repairs. One worker improved the slack time by getting married.

OCTOBER 30.   The well drillers came back in full force, three cars of them, with the new bride. They were married over the weekend.

NOVEMBER 1.   The drillers struck water at 148 feet at a barrel a minute. The well has 113 feet of water in it.

NOVEMBER 13.   Willie went to Augusta and bought a new truck. $800.

DECEMBER 2.   It has been very warm. Winnowed 140 bushels of beans.

DECEMBER 6.   The wildcat came tonight at 12 o'clock and again at 1:30. Terrible noise. He has not been here since a year ago in October.

DECEMBER 8.   Mrs. Effie Minot died this A.M. at 4 o'clock, aged 103 years and 22 days.

DECEMBER 10.   Our first snow. George shot our wild heifer today.

DECEMBER 16.   Brought home new Chevrolet truck today.

DECEMBER 25.   We all had a very merry Christmas.

1940

JANUARY 6.   This is Dorothy's birthday. She is 28 years old. It was 40 below zero and 4 feet of snow on the ground the day she was born.

JANUARY 10.   I have felt some better today and have worked on the Mills genealogy. It is very interesting. Willie took a load of wood to Augusta and got 400 lbs. of sugar at $4.90 and 4 barrels of flour.

Maggie Wilson from Nova Scotia called. We had a great talk. I haven't seen her for 33 years. Maggie and I played Chinese checkers. Lots of fun.

FEBRUARY 6. The 7½ horse power motor came today. Motor and wiring $255.25. We sawed wood with it all day. It works fine.

MARCH 5. Willie and I went to town meeting. It was a big jamboree. I hate the arguments.

Andrew Rowe, Willie and I went to see "Gone With the Wind". It was great.

APRIL 17. We papered the kitchen. Turned the curtains other end up, and they look like new. George delivered five loads of wood today. The wildcat came. I saw him real plain.

APRIL 20. We did general Saturday work, then Jean and I went to Augusta and bought a new couch at Diplocks, and he sent it right up. The men are pleased with it.

APRIL 24. George, Andy and Willie are surveying. Making a map of the farm. They have a good instrument that once belonged to Kennebec County.

MAY 6. Willie set out 20 apple trees on the Manley Knowles place. In the afternoon he went to Augusta and got a new two-row corn planter.

MAY 25. Turned out cows for the first time.

JUNE 14.. After dinner Willie and I started for Portland. We went to see the flag day parade and then to a movie.

We went to York Harbor, to see Aunt Eliza, who is 95 years old, and then to Ogunquit, to see her niece, Nella, who is 60. Nella's husband, Mr. Weare, was a contractor and built houses in Ogunquit. He was in one of these keeping a fire to dry plaster the night the steamer "Portland" went down.

JULY 21. Sunday. Went to Sunday School and church. This is our 31st wedding anniversary. The wildcat came and Andy went out but couldn't get a shot.

JULY 28. We got up a big dinner as Dorothy was coming from Lewiston where she had gone to attend the wedding of a very dear friend. But at the last moment it was postponed and never came off.

AUGUST 29. Frank Farnham came over with his tractor and threshed 300 bushels of barley.

SEPTEMBER 2. Dot and Ken came this P.M. on their way to the World's Fair in New York. Dot brought me a birthday present of a bird feeder.

SEPTEMBER 6. Had a letter from Dorothy at World's Fair. Willie went to Rockland for lime.

SEPTEMBER 8. A very busy day. Went to church and Sunday School, and then home and got dinner, and at 2:30 Dot and Ken came back from the World's Fair, and had so much to talk about. At 4:30 they had to start for Bar Harbor.

SEPTEMBER 12. The wild cat came and Andy fired at him, but missed. George hauled the old tractor to the junk dealer. Got $21 for it. It was 23 years old.

SEPTEMBER 12. Everyone is all ready for the wildcat tonight. A neighbor had one of his cows badly injured by a bull moose last night.

OCTOBER 6. George and Reita were married at 8:30 P.M. Mrs. Lord drove the Buick, and she and I went down to South Gardiner to the wedding, and they started on their honeymoon.

OCTOBER 7. Had a telephone call from Kenneth that Dorothy is very sick and in the hospital.

OCTOBER 8. Dorothy is very sick but some better tonight. I have been so worried all day. I do hope and pray that poor Dorothy may be better tomorrow. It is so hard to have her sick and not be able to go to her.

OCTOBER 9. We have not heard from Dorothy today, but we are hoping.

OCTOBER 16. The men put running water in the barn today. Had card from Ken saying that Dot was better. Have felt quite well today. Have lost 14 lbs. during the last 4 weeks.

Had a letter from Ken, and Dot doesn't seem much better, am so worried. Lila Mansfield called tonight and said Dorothy was better. We hope and pray she is.

OCTOBER 18. Had a card from Kenneth saying that Dorothy seems a little better. I went to the hospital for another treatment. Pretty tough. Willie went over to Elmer Dunn's to look at the old Penney settlement.

OCTOBER 22. Good news from Dorothy today.

OCTOBER 26. Not a very good day. A Mr. Quimby ran into our car and damaged it quite a lot. Then we came home, after my treatment at the hospital, and Ken called me up and said that Dorothy was worse and had gone to the operating room. Called later and said she was easier.

OCTOBER 27. Got up early and George and I went to Bar Harbor to see Dorothy. How sick she looked. I stayed with her for two or three minutes. Got home at 6:15 P.M. I stood the trip fine. Our poor dog Bobby lost an eye today. We don't know how it happened.

OCTOBER 28. Poor Dorothy is not so well tonight, and we are worried.

OCTOBER 29. Willie and I left Belgrade at 1:30 P.M. and got to Bar Harbor at 4:45. Ken came home and at 7 we went to the hospital. Dot looks better than she did Sunday.

OCTOBER 30. Got up and had a good breakfast and all seemed so happy that Dot was better, but at 11:15 she had a bad turn and at 11:30 she passed away, was gone when we got there. Willie and I left Bar Harbor at 12:30. A sad trip home.

OCTOBER 31. A very sad day. We have had many telephone calls. Everyone is so nice and thoughtful to us.

NOVEMBER 1. The hardest day I have ever lived. We laid poor little Dorothy away to rest today. She had the most wonderful flowers I ever saw. The house just full of them, and so many people all so sympathetic and sorry for us. Everyone loved her.

NOVEMBER 2. Another hard day without Dorothy. We had many lovely cards and notes of sympathy.

NOVEMBER 3. Another hard day. We all went to the cemetery. The flowers looked fine after the rain.

NOVEMBER 4. We washed and I made 4 sofa pillows and three meat loaves. The wildcat is howling now at 8:45, early for him. Ken did not call today.

NOVEMBER 5. Ken came this A.M. and stayed to dinner, then left Dorothy's trunk and started for Bar Harbor. Willie and I went up to vote at noon, and then looked over the things in Dorothy's trunk. Such a sad job.

NOVEMBER 12. It has been a very rainy day. Five more cards of sympathy, 54 now.

NOVEMBER 13. Went to Ladies' Aid at Eda Gowell's. Passed in 6 aprons for our table at the Fair.

NOVEMBER 14. We went to Bar Harbor for Dorothy's things, a hard trip and hard to have all her things brought home.
.... Ken came about 10:30 and we went up to the cemetery to see Dorothy's monument.

NOVEMBER 20. Finished my blue silk dress. This A.M. at 2:30 there was an earthquake, quite severe. It shook the house and made things rattle. We took a nice Xmas tree over to the Tripps, all loaded with presents.

1941

JANUARY 6. This was Dorothy's birthday, and it has been a very hard day. Joan Stuart came down on the school bus. I am going to make a dress for her.

JANUARY 19. The wildcat came last night right to the corner of the house. Willie whistled and he answered back. Have worked on pictures tonight, putting names on them and getting them ready for album.

JANUARY 24. Went for a long walk, then picked up some of Dot's things.

FEBRUARY 10. This is Harry's birthday. We made him a cake, and took him a boiled dinner and a picture of Dorothy in a frame.

FEBRUARY 21. Jean and I deloused 64 hens in 35 minutes tonight. Willie and I went to Augusta. He got a new overcoat, and it looks fine.

FEBRUARY 28. Sewed on aprons all day for the Ladies' Aid. February has been an extraordinary month. Less than one eighth inch of snow. The least in 70 years.

MARCH 2. I read and studied Town Report. Willie and I went up to vote. They elected the same officers as last year.

APRIL 4. Talk about wildcats, he came seven times last night. I took 47 dozen eggs to Augusta and got .25 and .30 cents for them.

APRIL 19. Jean Robinson went home for the last time. I shall miss her. Chas. Thurstin and wife came to work.

MAY 30. We went to the cemetery with flowers. A very stirring day. We had 15 callers.

JUNE 10. George went to Ogunquit this P.M. to get Aunt Eliza and her things. She stood the trip well.

JUNE 21. Very, very hot. 102 in the sun. The 6 men got in 5 loads of hay.

JULY 10. George and Reita have an 8½ lb. baby girl at 10:00 A.M. George and I went in to see the baby tonight. They have named it Sandra Dorothy.

JULY 14. They took down the old windmill today that pumped water for us for 50 years, and what a job! Margaret and I picked blueberries.

JULY 16. Almost done haying, 103 loads. There will be about 3 more to get.

AUGUST 15. Canned 6 quarts of apples and 6 quarts of mustard pickles. That makes 245 now. I took the Buick to Augusta. I left the Buick at the garage and went to the hospital for a treatment. Then we came home and got dinner for 6 men. Frank Farnham helped thresh.

SEPTEMBER 15. Aunt Eliza is 96 years old today. We got the new Farmall tractor today.

SEPTEMBER 25. Sandra was sick, and I went down to help give her castor oil. She didn't like it.

.... Had a nice time at Farm Bureau. Gipsies camped here, but the Sheriff drove them off.

OCTOBER 31. Chester and Clarence started work on the new walk-in refrigerator.

NOVEMBER 7. We paid our taxes today, $328.16.

DECEMBER 7. Did not go to church today. I did not feel like driving the car, and Willie could not go. They say over the radio that the Japs have declared war on the United States.

DECEMBER 8. War is declared on Japan today. Everyone is pretty much worried. I did two weeks washing today and finished an apron. The masons came and plastered the refrigerator, and men took down the old Farmers' telephone line that was put up 28 years ago. I did a big ironing, had the henhouse cleaned out, and did a lot of work down there.

DECEMBER 20. A very busy day. The men loaded a car with pulpwood, and I wrapped and labeled over 500 lbs. of beef and pork.

DECEMBER 21. I went to the biggest wedding Belgrade has seen. I met a lot of nice people and had a fine time.

1942

JANUARY 6. This is Dorothy's birthday. She would have been 30. Farnham's barn caught fire, but it was put out without much damage.

JANUARY 25. Willie did a lot of soldering on milk cans, and I got a lot of things ready for the Red Cross. Some job.

.... A very stormy day. The school bus got stuck, and the men had to get the team and haul it out. George was appointed air raid warden for the district today.

APRIL 2. Assessors called.

APRIL 4. Seven county agents were here today to look at our electrical equipment.

APRIL 9. I got my new Bulova watch today. It is a dear.

APRIL 12. About ten inches of snow came, and cars have been getting stuck on the hill all day. Too bad when it was so dry.

APRIL 15. We all went up to the Depot to see Ken McKenzie and his gang of entertainers. It was quite good but not so good as the last time.

APRIL 27. They chopped down the old plumb trees.

.... Willie and I took Aunt Eliza to have her eyes fitted for glasses. Official blackout tonight. Willie and George went down to Monmouth and bought a horse.

MAY 24. They took the new horse, "Dooley," for weighing and found that she weighs 1970 lbs. She is black, slick and handsome.

MAY 29. Willie moved the Hearne family into the Will Watson place. There are 12 of them, and the bedbugs were simply numberless. I went to the cemetery and decorated seven lots.

MAY 31. A heavy frost. Killed everything that was not covered.

JUNE 14. Sunday. A big day. Lydia Farnham and Albert Johnson were married and came down to the Farnhams for the reception. A big affair. I helped to arrange the flowers and did not go to church.

JUNE 18. Did some shopping at Gowell's, and this evening have set out a lot of plants.

JUNE 22. I hustled around and got my work done, as Sandra was coming up. She stayed until 4:30, was real good.

JULY 14. Three terrible thunder showers. The fireworks were awful, our lights were out for half an hour.

.... The State nurse was here, and says they may take the Fowler children to the Good Will Farm. Willie and I went to Augusta, and I got Gloria and Betty Tripp new shoes, stockings, ribbons and bloomers, and slips. George got a new job today chauffeuring for Mr. Adams at the Lakes.

.... Willie discovered that milk was being stolen, so he had to put a lock on the tank.

AUGUST 7. Finished haying, 175 loads. It has been a very difficult season, with much rain and poor help, 6 men, when they felt like coming. 55 days from the start.

AUGUST 28. My birthday. Many cards and snapshots. Belgrade has had a clearing out, Clarence and his 3 children and the Hearnes, 12, have left.

SEPTEMBER 12. Went to church and Sunday school with the usual passengers. I took flowers to Ray Hammond, who is sick.

SEPTEMBER 15. We had Aunt Eliza down to spend her 97th birthday.

SEPTEMBER 23. Willie took his dinner and went to haul lime for Mr. Bradley in Rome. The boys took the team and went to haul logs for a neighbor, so I am alone.

OCTOBER 5. A large blimp or Zeppelin went over today. The story is that it broke loose in Boston. Miss Mary Buzzell and her class in home economics in the high school are coming down here tomorrow to see the refrigerator.

OCTOBER 12. I had a big surprise. Reita expects a baby in 4 months. How I hope it is a boy. We need him on the farm. Sandra walked all the way up from the other house alone today. She is 15 months old.

OCTOBER 16. Willie's birthday. He is 60.

OCTOBER 27. Have just had my first Christmas present. A war bond from Willie. We have bought 9 this year.

NOVEMBER 5. Charles Pomroy came back tonight, real drunk.

79

NOVEMBER 12. Ray Hammond, our mail man for many years, died last night.

NOVEMBER 29. Charles went to Augusta yesterday and got soused. He stayed in bed all day.

NOVEMBER 30. Charles' brother came and got him. The bed was soaked.

DECEMBER 2. Had a letter from our old milk tester, Albert Bennett. He says that he and his buddies can operate their gun so·as to have two shells in the air at the same time.

DECEMBER 20. Aunt Eliza fell and cut her head, and Willie went up. We got our man, Chester, deferred from the draft today.

.... The end of the old year. I have canned 690 quarts. I have made 23 aprons, 18 dresses, 12 prs. bloomers, 9 slips, and 5 nighties.

1943

JANUARY 1. No mail. I cooked.

JANUARY 15. No help. Willie fired Chet and hired two Strickland boys, to come Monday.

JANUARY 18. One of the boys came. George came home sick. The new man is very slow and quiet. I think this has been the most terrible day I can remember, so cold and such an awful wind. The roads are not broken and the milk had to be taken out to the main road with the horses. The new man walked to the Depot and took the train to Waterville, where he had a case in court.

JANUARY 22. The Strickland boys went home on "business," and Willie was without help for one day.

FEBRUARY 4. The Belgrade High School building burned flat last night. A terrible thing, such a big loss. Everyone is just sick. Sandra is quite sick, and I am worried, temperature 103.

FEBRUARY 15. George and Reita have a baby girl named Donna Mary.

MARCH 8. Went down to the other house to see Donna Mary for the first time.

* APRIL 20. The ground is covered with snow. Lawrence and Omah Strickland swapped cars again. We think that they are in some kind of trouble, as one of them said, "We can't be good, but we can be careful."

APRIL 26. The last snow left the cow lane. Clarence plowed all day. Saw two deer in the field below the other house.

---

* March 24. At noon I went to Estabrook Hall to the Outstanding Homemakers' and Farmers' Banquet, and was chosen Chief Homemaker. I also went to the dairy meeting where I received a $45.00 prize for Willie from Hood Co. as the result of his increasing average herd production 1946 lb.

MAY 11. We listened to John Hasey over the radio tonight at 8 o'clock. He is the son of Willie's cousin, Helen Penney, and is reported to be the first casualty of the Second World War. He was in the French Foreign Legion.

MAY 14. I went to the observation post and spotted eight planes. Willie bought a pig for $25.00.

MAY 25. Turned the cows, heifers, and hens out for the first time. Mabel and I went to the observation post. Our replacement came late, the worst for beer.

JULY 15. We heard last night that Ernest Rutter has been killed in action overseas. Ruth and Miriam Wort came to pick strawberries.

JULY 22. Just got to sleep, when there was a call for a blackout, and George had to go down the road and black them out.

JULY 23. Had Dr. Reynolds last night and again today. He says I came near having pneumonia, but am better tonight.

JULY 24. Have had a real uncomfortable day. Laura and all the kiddies are here. She is a dear.

JULY 25. Sunday. Left home in the Knowlton and Hewins ambulance, and they put me in the Sturgis room on ward 10. Mrs. Polly is my nurse.

JULY 26. Had a pretty good night, except I fell out of bed.

AUGUST 3. Dr. said I could go home, so Willie came down. Home at 12:30, and it did seem good.

AUGUST 28. My birthday. We took Clarence's two daughters to Good Will Farm.

NOVEMBER 9. Willie and Lawrence Minot went to Oakland to a creamery meeting. It seems that there has been an error in collecting samples of the milk at the creamery, and Willie was the first to discover it, thanks to the official testing we were doing. Willie got a $776.36 adjustment. Others who had records, were paid according to the amount delivered.

NOVEMBER 27. Valentine McKackeny called for honey. What an odd name?

DECEMBER 14. My half sister, Gertie Dudley, passed away today. She was the mother of 14 children.

JANUARY 1. A quiet day. This evening I have sewed on aprons. I made 4 pies this P.M.

JANUARY 6. Aunt Eliza is quite sick. We had Dr. Williams for her. Willie went up to see her.

JANUARY 11. Aunt Eliza passed away at 8:30 P.M. in her 100th year.

.... We went to Aunt Eliza's funeral. The minister recounted the inventions and discoveries made during her long life.

FEBRUARY 5. We had a cow bred artificially today.

FERBUARY 15. Finished Mina's two aprons and cut out an apron and a dress for myself. The snow is so deep and they say more is coming. Poor Bert Farnham is not so well.

FEBRUARY 25. We hired a new man today, Emery Kelley.

MARCH 6. Town Meeting today. I went but it was very tiresome.

APRIL 7. I went to Farmingdale with Willie, and called on the Fletchers, while Willie went on to Bowdoinham for fertilizer. When we got home two officers were here to tell us about Elmer Ellsworth, who had forged three checks on us totaling $159.00, and they have him in jail.

.... A flock of wild geese lit in our field, and stayed for two hours. Had a cow butchered.

APRIL 26. Had a letter from Ted Newell, from out west, one of our first hired men. He wanted to know about his family. Some of his relatives called, and we were able to bring him up to date.

MAY 19. Went to Augusta and met Helen Hasey and her husband. She is Willie's cousin, and he is the traveling supervisor for Walkover shoes. Had a nice time talking with them about old times and looking over old things.

JUNE 6. The European invasion started in the night. Started haying. Willie went to Lewiston for the trial of Ellsworth, the forger.

JUNE 16. Our first artificially bred calf was born.

JUNE 30. Laura and the kiddies came over this P.M.

JULY 31. Took Dot Tripp home to stay.

SEPTEMBER 6.   Mrs. Lillian Penney Low came from Vermont to pick up the missing link in the Penney family history. We helped all we could. Finished another dress for Caroline, and this evening made over a skirt for her. Emery has been cutting corn all day with the horses.

....   Finished filling the last silo. 10 little pigs came today and a calf.

OCTOBER 4.   Hustled all A.M. and went to Ladies' Aid in P.M. at Mrs. Simon Thing's. A big crowd out and we made plans for our fair. Alden shot a fox tonight.

DECEMBER 25.   Willie made me a Christmas present of $100.00.

DECEMBER 31.   The last day of the old year, and Willie and I are alone. I have made this year 47 aprons, 1 skirt, 19 dresses, 7 slips, 3 prs. bloomers, 9 pillows, 2 holders, and 8 sheets, and I have put up more than 500 jars of canned goods.

1946

JANUARY 15. Billy Burke, a boy from Newfoundland, is with us now, and he is good. He arrived in Augusta very early one morning in a group of 30, to help during the War. The County Agent and Willie were the only ones to meet them.

JANUARY 20. The roads are not broken, no mail, and no milk man. Emery delivered the milk with the horses.

.... I have written a letter to Sara Winslow, in the hospital. She was taken from here, when her husband worked for us. She is quite rational and can do wonders with a crochet needle. They lost their boy in the War.

.... The new sawmill arrived today.

FEBRUARY 23. The roads were broken in the night, and we got 3 days mail. The veterinary was here today. The last straw. All our cows have hemorrhagic septisemic.

FEBRUARY 25. Our milk production has been greatly reduced by this outbreak.

MARCH 14. Willie has been grafting his apple trees. Thelma Smith spent the P.M. with me, and I trimmed and made over two hats for her. Will Sawyer, a good mill man, has been here several days setting up our sawmill.

MARCH 22. They did the first sawing at the mill today. Our timber growing on the farm has been estimated at about half a million feet. The mill machinery and building represent an investment of about $5,000.

.... Our man, Emery Kelley, has just married Beverly Buker, and had the day off, but came back for chores. We have played Cupid for three boys we have brought into town, who have married local girls. I took the car out, the first time since last fall.

APRIL 23. William Poole, another boy from Newfoundland, came here to work today.

MAY 20. Put out the cattle for the first time today.

.... Got Mrs. Wilcox's dress ready to fit, and cut out a dress for Hazel.

JUNE 4. Caroline Mills came over and I fixed her evening dress and graduation dress.

JULY 1. Our men have got in 36 loads of hay.

JULY 4. Caroline came over and I finished two of her dresses and fixed two more.

AUGUST 1. We went to church and learned that poor little crippled Vida Sprague had passed away. We sang some hymns that she had picked out the Sunday before.

.... Caroline came over and did my work while I sewed for her. I have made her a plaid woolen dress, and shortened 3 skirts.

OCTOBER 18. Willie sold four cows today for $480.

NOVEMBER 3. Pulled a tooth for Sandra.

.... Washed, and sewed on Catherine's pajamas.

DECEMBER 25. Christmas and Willie and I were alone. We had a nice lot of presents.

.... Catherine came over and I shortened and fixed a dress for her, then cut out a skirt and finished it.

.... Sunday, and I have written 7 letters.

1947

JANUARY 10. We dressed a beef today, and took it up to Ken Bartlett's to have it cut up.

FEBRUARY 1. A wonderful day. I finished two dresses for Alberta Yeaton.

FEBRUARY 25. Catherine came over, and I have sewed for her all day on a pink dress for the play.

MARCH 3. Town meeting day. Willie and I were on the dinner committee.

MARCH 13. We got word that Eva, Willie's sister, has passed away in Colorado.

MARCH 21. Celia Chaput came over and we got the paper off the kitchen and plastered two holes in the wall.

APRIL 7. Celia came over and we partly papered the kitchen. The men are sawing in the mill.

APRIL 21. Rosalind came and I made a dress for her, all but the hemming.

APRIL 22. Rosalind came and did the work, and I sewed for her, making another dress for her and most of a skirt.

MAY 3. My new bedroom furniture came. We replaced the wood cook stove with an electric one.

JUNE 19. The agricultural class at Belgrade High School are here tonight looking over the farm. The movie men, six of them, have been here all day taking pictures of the farm. We have the first field haybaler that has come into Belgrade, and they are setting it up today.

JUNE 30. Finished setting up the haybaler and started haying. The men have used the haybaler and pickup machine with good results.

AUGUST 6. Florrie and Stewart Robinson came from Halifax, Nova Scotia. I have not seen her for 41 years. We have talked a lot.

AUGUST 23. This P.M. Dan Brown called. He is Willie's cousin, and they went to school together.

.... In the evening Willie and I went to see "The Egg and I." It was very good.

SEPTEMBER 11. A bulldozer came and worked two hours. The site is being prepared for a new house.

DECEMBER 31. I guess it has been a pretty good year. During the year, I have made 10 prs. pajamas, 39 aprons, 26 dresses, 1 coat, 6 skirts, 5 pillow cases, 5 roller towels, 16 pillow ticks, 4 sheets, and 2 caps. (We sold from the woods during the years to date, pulpwood, fuel wood, and birch bolts to the amount of $19,140.00. The woodland has been a valuable source of income, and now with the sawmill it may be increased.)

1948

JANUARY 1. I figured that my hens made a profit of $78.89 last month. Willie went to see if Frank Pray would build our house, and was much encouraged.

JANUARY 30. Gandhi, the Indian leader, was shot today.

FEBRUARY 23. Rosalind came over and we did a big washing, then I cut out a nice dress for her.

.... Catherine came over and I made a dress for her. Finished Rosalind's dress. This week I have made 4 dresses and been away one day to the Farm Bureau. I have tried to maintain strict discipline in the Farm Bureau meetings.

.... We had a nice dinner at Town Meeting, but the scrapping and arguments were awful, and I didn't enjoy it one bit.

MARCH 22. Started the new house today. Frank Pray, Leslie Bickford, and Guy Yeaton came.

APRIL 23. Just home from hospital where we have been to see Willie, who got cut on the saw and lost 4 toes.

MAY 6. The carpenters went away tonight on another job. I went over and swept up. Clarence Day called. Willie and I went to Waterville and made arrangements to have inlaid linoleum for the house.

JUNE 5. Frank Bailey was here and brought me a lovely electric waffle iron and a toaster as a gift for letting them take my picture for the paper.

JUNE 25. Here we are moved into the new house.

JULY 13. What a night we had! The Pikes stole the truck and started for Augusta, but on the way they had an accident. Two officers came and took Pike and he got 60 days. Mrs. Pike came back with another man, but he went away, and Willie took her to Augusta with all her things.

.... The Sears order came, with the vacuum cleaner, but the table was broken.

SEPTEMBER 2. They started making the fish pond today with a bulldozer and 3 men.

.... At the fish pond project, they fired about 200 lbs. of dynamite to open a drain. We should have notified the near neighbors, as they were much startled.

NOVEMBER .... We all went to Arthur Cottle's funeral.

DECEMBER 31. In this very eventful year, we built the house and moved in. Then we built the dam and made the fish pond on the land bought from Merton Knowles, insulated the big house with many other things. During the year I have made 48 aprons, 22 dresses, 4 skirts, 5 towels, fixed over an evening gown, and made 2 men's woolen shirts, and I think about 500 jars of canned goods.

1949

JANUARY 1. Not a bit of snow on the ground.

JANUARY 7. A telegram from Cousin Helen that Fred had passed away.

.... The men are working in the woods.

FEBRUARY 15. Word came today that Dr. Reynolds has passed away. He spend all of his practicing life in Belgrade, and when he was called, we knew everything would be all right.

MARCH 3.   I went to prayer meeting at the Penney Memorial Church.

MARCH ....   I finished Catherine's evening dress, and tonight, with my help, she cut out another and we have it partly done.

JUNE ....   Willie got his boat that Will Sawyer made for him.

JULY ....   I paid off the men Saturday night, $170.00.

JULY ....   Dan Brown, Willie's cousin, came from Massachusetts. There is a big spring in our woods that he used to visit when he was a boy out hunting. He is feeble but he wanted to see it once more, so Willie went with him.

JULY 21.   This is our 40th wedding anniversary. Willie went to Rockland for lime, and got two big lobsters and two big fish.

AUGUST 4.   Put 580 trout in the pond. The children are here tonight. George is combining for Guy Yeaton.

AUGUST 8.   George is combining for Frank Farnham.

AUGUST 28.   This is my birthday and I am 63. A flying machine has been buzzing around all day, and landed in our fields. The Cotes went to Portland, and haven't got back tonight.

OCTOBER 19.   Our good neighbor, Bert Farnham, passed away.

NOVEMBER 8.   Dressed a cow that went wild and had to be shot.

DECEMBER 31.   The Cotes left this noon for Aroostook, and we were all so glad. They came March 13 and have been one headache.

1950

JANUARY 1.   No snow, warm.

JANUARY 4.   Washed out 32 jars that were left dirty in Cote's house, and 83 dirty fruit jars. Cedric and I cleaned kitchen and pantry, washed all dishes and cooking utensils. Some job.

JANUARY 22.   We have hired the milk tester, Oral Page, and his wife, Connie. They are moving into the other house.

FEBRUARY 2.   The men are working in the woods, cutting logs for a new barn.

FEBRUARY 8.   Cold, 32 below zero. Catherine came over and I fixed a dress for her.

MARCH 7.   Oral's birthday, so I made him a cake. Willie went to Thomaston today to buy some harnesses for the horses.

MARCH 12.   Oral and Connie have a 10 lb. and 4 ounce baby girl, Pamela Ann.

APRIL 2.   Willie and I made out the census questionnaire.

MAY 8.   Got a new tractor and had the Buick fixed up again.

....   Four of the Tripps came over tonight and hung George and Cedric a Maybasket.

AUGUST 1.   After supper, I took my first aeroplane ride with Lawrence Bigelow. Flew all over Belgrade. It was grand.

SEPTEMBER 5.   The bulldozer came today and is leveling the hill for the new barn.

OCTOBER 2.   The men commenced work on the foundation for the new barn.

OCTOBER 7.   Saturday. The men continued work on the foundation for the new barn.

NOVEMBER 4.   Oral Page, our hired man, got a deer. Last night 54 pullets had to be put on the roost, and tonight 32, so they are learning.

NOVEMBER 16.   Took Mabel and went to Catherine Mills' bridal shower.

NOVEMBER 26.   Got word that Joe Penney, Willie's nephew, had died.

DECEMBER 17.   Connie and Oral moved away today.

1952

JANUARY 10.   A busy day. Willie cut up a hog and I wrapped and labeled it, and made five dishes of hogshead cheese.

JANUARY 11.   Frank Farnham's house burned down at 1:15 A.M.

JANUARY 14.   Got up early and had my washing all done before the men came in to breakfast. The Farnhams moved some things into our house. Frank and Claudia worked at the big house all day.

JANUARY 17.   Frank Farnham and family moved into the big house this afternoon. We will not charge the Farnhams any rent at present.

FEBRUARY 18.   No milk man, no mail. The roads are full of snow and the radio says 31 inches had come at dark.

FEBRUARY 19.   George didn't get home last night or today. Just got the meals, as the children and Dawn have kept things lively.

FEBRUARY .... The snowplow wiggled through. They haven't had a road beyond here for a week.

MARCH 10. George and I went to Augusta and got a new red Buick.

MARCH 24. The men sawed lumber.

APRIL 19. First frogs sang, and Frank Farnham planted 1½ acres of peas.

MAY .... George brought home 4 big trout. We had them for dinner.

JUNE 2. Monday. This is the anniversary of the death of my school chum, Ethel Bird, who died at the age of 15.

JUNE 14. Willie and I went to Oakland. Had two blowouts coming home, which took the joy out of the trip.

JUNE 25. Willie's high school class of 1902 had their reunion here. Ten of the class were present.

JUNE 26. Went to Belgrade Depot and met Tom Mills, my cousin, whom I have not seen for many years, and we talked about old friends until midnight.

JULY.... George went bailing hay for Harry Alexander. I did not go anywhere, as it was so hot, 105 in the shade.

OCTOBER 16. Tonight Frank Farnham's store was broken into and $60.00 worth taken.

1953

FEBRUARY 11. More than 30 men came to the barn meeting, and they had a good two hours talk. Clifford Hilbert brought us a hot water heater for the barn.

FEBRUARY 20. Put a phone in the new barn, and it works well.

MARCH 4. The men sawed in the mill all day.

APRIL 9. Willie, Clayton and Otto set 1000 little pines over by the stream.

APRIL 21. The children came down and did the work, and I sewed for them, finishing their skirts, and they are so proud of them.

JUNE 9. Have been getting ready for my Nova Scotia trip.

JULY 5. I started from Waterville on June 13 at 3:20 A.M. for a three weeks visit to Nova Scotia, arriving at Spring Hill at 8:00 P.M. My cousin, Martha Simpson, who lives in Truro, had made me a nice visit in Belgrade, so I went to call on her first. The following day was Sunday, and Martha and I went to Church. The joy of meeting old friends and relatives, and seeing again the dear home surroundings, was as great as I have ever known. I went to Mapleton and took some pictures of my childhood home, which is unchanged. The elm trees, so large now that it shades the house, I planted when a girl. Everett Brown lives there now, and he asked if I would mind if he cut off a limb from this tree that was chafing the house. Then we went in to my father's sugar woods, and I found my name on a sap tub. I had not been there for 47 years. The cemetery is only a little way from the old home, and I visited my mother's grave that I may never see again. Every day I visited relatives and friends, or they called on me. I visited in the homes of 16 cousins and 25 dear friends of the old days, renewing acquaintances and talking over old times without end. Today we got up at 4:00 A.M. and started for Belgrade at 5:00. Stopped for lunch twice and arrived home at 5:30 P.M. 462 miles.

JULY 23. The men got all the hay in, about 10 tons.

AUGUST 1. I went to Howard Gowell's funeral. He has kept store in town many years and will be much missed. His brother, George, says there are several uncollectable store bills on his books of $1,000 or more.

SEPTEMBER 1. Leighton Castle called up from Florida and said that Cora is not so well, and wants Rose to come down, and she is going tomorrow.

An air view of the Penney farm about 1952.

SEPTEMBER 8. Had word from Florida that sister Cora had passed away. It is too sad for words.

SEPTEMBER 30. We got a new Holstein bull today.

OCTOBER 6. George shot 2 nice ducks and I dressed them.

.... George and Buker put new aluminum roof on grainery and big house ell.

OCTOBER .... The men put in the cement foundation for a new silo. It will be 18 feet by 41.

NOVEMBER 4. Took my second driving lesson this A.M. with the new Oldsmobile.

NOVEMBER 29. George came home with a nice 7 point buck. Been gone a week.

1954

JANUARY 23. We have our T.V. set in and it is working fine. Made blueberry muffins and watched T.V. a lot today.

JANUARY .... I got a call from Rose saying that Bessie had lost the sight of her other eye and is totally blind. George took me down and I have stayed with her all day and what a day. When she lost the sight of the first eye the oculist told her that she could save the other by a slight operation, and it seemed so necessary that he offered to do it for nothing. She refused his offer, trusting to Christian Science, and now she is blind. Her sister, Cora, had a cancer but put her trust in Christian Science. At last she consulted a surgeon. He told her, "You have waited too long, you may live 6 months."

MAY .... The men took their dinner and went to the woods, and I was alone all day. Fed the cattle and hens.

JUNE 30. Went to a birthday party for Ann Yeaton. There were present 4 old maids, 5 widows, and 2 women with husbands.

JULY .... A man from Cornell University and a professor from Colby called to see the farm and asked permission to collect turtles from our pond. They got plenty.

JULY 15. I went to the woolen mill and got a lot of rug material for Olive Spear, who is making the most wonderful braided rugs.

JULY 21. Dawn Farnham came over and returned 20 books. They are great readers.

AUGUST 31. What a day and it is still very bad. August went out with a bang, helped along by that terrible hurricane "Carol." We suffered the loss of telephone and electricity, and had to milk by hand with lanterns. We pumped water with a tractor, belting the power through a window.

SEPTEMBER 11. What a day! We listened on the radio to reports of that terrible hurricane "Edna," which hit here about 7:00 P.M., putting out the telephone and electricity.

SEPTEMBER 23. Dumped my fly bottles and buried 5 quarts of them. That makes 20 quarts of flies that I have buried this summer, and it has kept the three houses fly-free.

OCTOBER 16. George and I started for Needham, Massachusetts, at 7:30 A.M. It was raining hard but we got to Needham to see Rose at noon.

OCTOBER 17. Started for home from Needham at 3:10 P.M., stopping at Lewiston on the way. Betty and all her goods came with us.

NOVEMBER 4. 69 years today since my mother and father were married. She lived to be 38 and he lived to be 73. Mother's closing years were saddened by long illness.

NOVEMBER 9. Went to an all-day Farm Bureau meeting at North Belgrade. Had a delightful time.

DECEMBER 24. George has given Betty an engagement ring and she brought it to show me tonight. They are to be married on February 14th. I am overjoyed.

DECEMBER 25. George and Betty went for Bessie. We had a wonderful lot of presents. I have had 118 Christmas cards, and I have sent 120.

1955

JANUARY 24. They commenced putting milk in the new bulk tank. It has a 500 gallon capacity and cost $3,000.00.

FEBRUARY 12. The Farnham family moved out of the big house today and into John Wadleigh's house.

FEBRUARY 14. Monday. An all-important day. George and Betty were married. It was a lovely wedding, and they got away without much trouble.

FEBRUARY 18. 15 inches of snow and everything is covered deep.

FEBRUARY 20. George and Betty are back from their wedding trip.

APRIL 19. Willie went to Augusta with the old milk tank, sold to Hood Co. for $300.00. Went to the Depot with eggs and got .10 cents per lb. for parsnips.

MAY 30. Willie and George went up and brought Harry down to stay with George and Betty.

JUNE 5. This is the birthday of Ethel Bird, my childhood chum, who died in 1902.

JUNE .... I stayed with Harry while George and Betty went to Sandra's graduation.

SEPTEMBER 28. George is 36 years old today.

NOVEMBER 24. Thursday. George took Betty to the hospital, and they have a baby girl, Pamela Joyce Penney. A happy Thanksgiving.

NOVEMBER 27. I went with George to get Betty and the baby. I held her all the way home, she is so cute and good. She weighs 6 lbs., 11 oz.

DECEMBER 28. Betty brought Pamela over for her first visit. She is five weeks old.

.... During 1955 I have made 73 aprons, 9 dresses, 4 bibs, and one cap. Receipts from milk $11,538, pulp wood $794.62, fuel $315.20, livestock $718.00. We were making extensive improvements which left us with a profit of only $529.56. This year Willie put 96½ tons of lime on the fields, which is much needed.

1956

JANUARY .... 24 below zero.

JANUARY 6. Dorothy would have been 44 years old today.

JANUARY 20. Betty had an automatic washer and drier put in.

JANUARY 28. Carl Batchelder came in with blood all over him. He had gotten hurt in the woods, and I had to take him to Dr. Fenwick in Oakland.

FEBRUARY 7. About a foot of snow came in the night and roads not broken all day.

FEBRUARY 10. Pamela had a cold and we took her to the doctor.

FEBRUARY 17. Gould Rogers and General Hill called for eggs. During the Second World War, General Hill was our representative in Russia, part of whose business it was to care for our airmen who had to land there. He found the Russian women were as rugged as the men, and worked as hard. His Russian chauffeur would drive right into crowds and when General Hill remonstrated, said, "Let them get out of the way." Once his chauffeur seemed to lack interest in his work. On inquiry it turned out that that was the only day he was supposed to have off in the whole year. On an occasion when General Hill wanted to take a bath, two girls were sent in to give him a massage. They were surprised at his objections and said "That is the way we do here."

APRIL 20. Got word that Willie's Aunt Carrie Penney passed away last night.

MAY 3. Heard tonight that a Belgrade boy, Ernest Wyman, had been killed.

JUNE 8. Got my fly bottles out and saw first whippoorwill.

JULY 3. Started haying. The men put clover in the silo and bailed some. Hugh Godfrey came tonight and is going to help us hay. He may board with us.

JULY 21. 47 years today since we were married. Willie and George went to Elizabeth Arden's auction, but bought nothing.

AUGUST 4. Big fire at the Lakes. The Hortense Hersom house burned.

AUGUST 18. They finished haying today. Pamela has been good, but I lifted her too much and hurt my back.

SEPTEMBER 10. Election day and all six of us went up to vote. Betty and I went to Waterville for repairs for the corn cutter.

OCTOBER 3. The Belgrade Lakes Hotel burned. It had been closed for the season, and the caretaker said he could have put out the fire if the water hadn't been shut off.

OCTOBER 6. The men got in 12 wild heifers today, but there are a lot more.

OCTOBER 17. Betty, Pamela and I went over to the back field and found the 23 black heifers, but they got away.

JANUARY 1. 24 below zero.

FEBRUARY 15. George and Betty started for Boston at 2:45 A.M. I have not done a thing all day but get the meals and play with Pamela. Hope I don't spoil her. Pamela was good all the time she was with me.

FEBRUARY 28. The men sawed in the mill today, the first time this year. Mr. Richards is a good sawyer. Saw the first crow.

APRIL 1. I took care of Pamela while Betty and the Lundgrens went to Orono. She was real good until John Lundgren came from school, and he acted so badly that she got real excited, and I had a hard time.

APRIL 13. Willie, Betty and I had to go to Grange, as I was to be honored for 50 years of membership and receive my gold certificate.

AUGUST 6. Emptied the fly bottles again, making 21 full quarts this season in all.

AUGUST 15. Mr. Richards took his oxen to Skowhegan Fair and got 3rd prize in pulling.

NOVEMBER 1. Willie and I went over back. He wanted me to see a big land improvement project that he has been working on for two weeks with two trucks and a power shovel. They have removed 60½ rods of stone wall. Now, with the exception of an oak, there is no obstruction in our 200 acres of fields.

DECEMBER 3. Betty sold her puppy for $35.00.

DECEMBER 23. Worked hard getting ready for Christmas. The Richards family came up and got their presents.

DECEMBER 24. This evening we will all go over to Betty's to open our presents.

DECEMBER 25. They all came over here to dinner. Harry was down, and we had everything that is right and proper for Christmas.

DECEMBER .... Ed Wadleigh's house and barn burned. He lives a little more than a mile from us. He lost 6 cows. A high wind caused a wire to come loose and fall on the barn, starting the fire.

1958

JANUARY 3. I got Willie Mills' birth certificate, that I have been working on since last March.

JANUARY 20. I have made 11 aprons for Mrs. Sahagian, and she seemed well pleased.

FEBRUARY 17. Tripp came over and said that Laura has cancer of the brain and cannot live.

FEBRUARY 18. I took Harold Tripp to Lewiston to see Laura. She is failing fast.

MARCH 1. The first crow, and he spent the night in George's garage.

MARCH 13. Laura Tripp passed away.

JUNE 11. Pamela is staying here tonight, and what a time I had to get her to sleep at 10.

JUNE 24. The men started haying.

JULY 5. It is just six years today since I came home from my 3 weeks visit to Nova Scotia.

AUGUST 1. Our old house in Sidney was burned to the ground today.

DECEMBER 24. We went over to George's and opened our presents, and what a lot, especially for dear little Pamela.

1959

JANUARY 10. Willie fell 5 times in getting to the barn. Awful slippery.

FEBRUARY 2. Willie is still lame from his falls.

MAY 13. We went to the cemetery to Aunt Annie Penney's committal service. She is the last of her generation.

JUNE 14. Raining but we went to Mary Tilton's wedding, and to the reception at the hall. Both places were packed. I never saw such a big wedding.

JULY 4. The men got in 20 loads of hay today.

JULY 18. The men are still working in the field haying at 8:45 P.M.

JULY 21. This is our golden wedding day. George and Betty took us out to supper, then to the Grange Hall at 8:00 P.M. What a surprise, when we got there! The hall was full and everything ready for a big celebration. We had several presents and $100.00 in cash.

JULY 29. It is 100 in the shade. I worked on my scrapbooks. A porcupine has been in our corn, and Willie has set some traps.

AUGUST 19. We had a most dreadful thunder shower this P.M. One of our best heifers was killed by lightning. She was all ready to freshen. It is lucky our buildings are rodded.

AUGUST .... Have written 120 thank-you notes to those who honored our golden wedding anniversary. It has been quite a job, as I wrote notes with many.

AUGUST 28. Betty and George went to a dog show in Waterville and got a lot of prizes and ribbons.

SEPTEMBER 27. Mr. and Mrs. Cecil Fitch and two children moved into the other house, and I sincerely hope they will be the best help we have ever had. I went down and called on the Fitches and their two little girls.

DECEMBER 25. A very wonderful Christmas. Willie and I went over and had dinner with George and Betty and Uncle Harry. A lovely dinner.

1960

JANUARY 15. Willie and I went to Oakland for groceries, and got 10 axes of ours that had new bits put on.

FEBRUARY 3. A lot of snow came last night, and the wind piled it in heaps.

FEBRUARY 6. Two men from the Augusta Supply Co. brought my new freezer, and I am so proud of it.

MARCH 24. George, Betty, Pamela, Willie and I went to Benton to a very special extension meeting, where Willie and George were honored as outstanding farmers. A plaque was presented to them, and we had our pictures taken.

MARCH 28. Made a report for the census taker.

APRIL 9. Sawed lumber for Carl Lundgren.

MAY 27. Betty sold another dog for $75.00.

JUNE 6. The men have had their supper, and Willie is harrowing, George is mowing, and Cecil is cultivating the garden.

JUNE 26. Willie got a bad cut over his eye 2½ inches long. Dr. Micheau stitched it up. It was a narrow escape for his eye.

JULY 27. George, Willie and I went to Harry Knowles' funeral in Augusta. He was our nearest neighbor.

OCTOBER 10. We closed the church for the winter. Every child got a present, and Ronald Alexander hadn't missed a Sunday, so he got a nice Bible with his name on it in gold letters.

NOVEMBER 4. We have 58 cows and 7 heifers to freshen soon, and with the young cattle, 112 in all.

NOVEMBER 18. A horse and wagon went by, something that hasn't happened in many years. Our dog nearly burst his throat barking.

DECEMBER 1. I filled all the water cans in the registers. It is quite a job to get down on your knees when you are old.

DECEMBER 17. We are worried a lot about Harry. He seems all mixed up and doesn't know what he is doing.

1961

JANUARY .... Cecil, our hired man, has gone to get his teeth fitted. He had to make several trips for this purpose, for as long as he did not have money enough, they had a pretext to do more work on them, and when he did get them, he put them in brush cleaner which dissolved the plates.

JANUARY 17. I sold my hens today. I only had 46, but I shall miss them, as it is the first time in 51 years that I have not had any hens. I can't take care of them.

FEBRUARY 2. Sent a letter to Gould Rogers who is in the hospital.

MARCH 4. Town Meeting, but I did not go. They elected the same officers.

JUNE 17. They commenced haying.

AUGUST 4. A bad shower stopped haying with 8 loads out.

AUGUST 13. No callers but Tripp, and he was real drunk.

SEPTEMBER 14. George, Betty and Pamela started for Nova Scotia at 5:00 tonight to stay over the weekend.

DECEMBER 25. Willie and I were alone. In canning this year I have done about 300 jars, and I have made 40 aprons. It has been rather a hard year.

FEBRUARY 6. Charley Mills called and showed us 2 long reels of farm machinery in operation.

APRIL 29. Harry has given his house to Jessie, and they are cleaning it out today.

MAY 10. Saw Harry. He seems fine.

MAY 20. Mrs. Judkins and I went down to the Longfellow greenhouse. Alden Longfellow worked for us 15 years ago. Now he has a fine home and 5 nice children.

JUNE 10. Alden Longfellow and his family called and stayed to supper.

JUNE 13. They started haying today with 3 new men.

MAY 6. Willie went to an ear specialist who took a lot of wax out of his ear. That operation upset his balancing ability, so he came out supported on both sides, as he trembled and tottered along. If Betty hadn't been there to lead him away, he might have been locked up.

JULY 22. Willie and I went to church and Sunday School. I had 4 in my class and, as it turned out, it proved to be the end of my Sunday School teaching after 64 years.

JULY 29. The men got in 15 loads of hay. Frank Farnham broke his leg today.

AUGUST 1. Earl Lovejoy, who worked 8 years for us when we were first married, visited us today. He knew all about photography, and it is to his help at that time that we are indebted for the great number of photos that we have now.

1963

JANUARY 1. The old house burned down tonight. It was 128 years old.

FEBRUARY 4. Willie and I made all the property over to George today.

FEBRUARY 18. The men are working on the new house.

MARCH 19. We got word that Harry had passed away.

MARCH 21. We went to poor Harry's funeral. It seems strange that Willie and I, the oldest members of two large families, are the only ones left alive, with one exception.

APRIL 11. I had a nice book from the University of Maine, with pictures of those who have been honored in the past, my photo was among the rest.

MAY 4. Willie rebuilt the shop chimney today. He got me a nice bundle of Mayflowers.

JULY 12. I have worked so hard today that I am too tired to go to Sandra's wedding. Sorry.

JULY 27. Jessie, Willie and I went to visit the place in Rome where we used to pasture our young cattle and tap the big rock maples. Of the nice camp we had 50 years ago, only a few sticks were left. In the short time we had, Willie could not find the place where we boiled the sap, it was so grown up. He was much disappointed.

AUGUST 23. Two Mormon ministers called on me today, but I told them I had been a Methodist for 60 years, and I didn't care to change.

OCTOBER 3. The men moved my poor old henhouse away to store wood at the new house. How I miss it! I kept hens in it for 50 years and made a lot of money.

OCTOBER 11. We went to a reunion of Willie's high school class of 1902. There were only 5 present, and it may be the last.

NOVEMBER 30. A powerful wind blew our old woodshed down. It was 40 feet long and 20 wide. A very useful building.

DECEMBER 25. A very quiet Christmas. Willie and I were alone. We got many presents and 83 cards.

1964

JANUARY 25. I have done quite a lot of cleaning, but I had to stop. So tired.

FEBRUARY 18. I have been working all day on my family history book. I think it is going to be nice.

FEBRUARY .... Still working on the Mills-Penney history books. Quite a job.

MARCH 21. Willie has made a nice cherry book case and put it up in the den.

APRIL 10. This would have been my dear Mother's birthday.

AUGUST .... I went to church taking my night-blooming cereus. It is a curiosity and a big fuss was made over it.

102

AUGUST 30. Went to church and met a lot of summer guests and had a nice time.

SEPTEMBER 20. Went to church and was very tired when I got home.

DECEMBER 24. We went over to the Christmas tree at the other house. George came for us with the car.

DECEMBER 29. My father would have been 100 years old today.

1965

JANUARY 4. Leslie Bickford died today. He was respected by all.

APRIL 5. Willie walked over to the place my family moved into when we came to Maine in 1906. It was burned years ago and is now up to bushes.

JUNE 20. Jessie visited us. She has been doing all the work in her daughter's house, while they both worked. It was too hard for her. She lost 20 lbs. and looks as if she had escaped from a fort reduced by famine.

JUNE 21. We were glad to get a visit by our old hired man, Andrew Rowe, and family.

JULY 2. The little catbirds have left their nest in the honey-suckle outside our bedroom window. I shall miss them. Mr. Hugh Godfrey and family called. He worked for us 12 years ago.

AUGUST 2. Bruce Gullion, a boy who worked for us 20 years ago, visited us with his family.

AUGUST 31. I am in bed most of the time. Pamela comes in and helps me. She is a dear.

OCTOBER 28. 40 little girls came down from school to see the cows and barns. During the past year I have canned 203 jars of preserves.

1966

JANUARY 3. Enough snow came last night to make the ice very slippery.

MARCH 8. We had quite a surprise. Our first hired man, Ray Nesbit, called.

MARCH 20. Did some reading, but most of the time I looked over old photos and snapshots that I haven't seen for many years.

One of about thirty rocking chairs made by Will Penney in his retirement.

APRIL 17.   How I wish I could feel as I used to. Dr. Morris just couldn't find anything wrong with me except the old arthritis.

MAY 1.   A crowd with a Maybasket for Pamela.

MAY 27.   Betty and I went to the cemetery with flowers for Harry and Dorothy.

MAY 30.   I gave Pamela her great-grandmother's watch. It is a nice one, and she is so pleased.

JUNE 23.   Poor Bessie passed away at 5:20.

JULY 27.   We sent a get-well card to our neighbor, Freeman Rowe, in the hospital.

AUGUST 15.   Cyrus Tobin called twice. He is a man who walks the road every day, and some think he isn't very bright.

AUGUST 24.   While waiting for Betty at the store, I met a lady who came from Canada, and we had a nice talk. It seems so good to meet anyone from Canada.

AUGUST 28.   My 80th birthday. I never expected to live so long.

AUGUST ....   Cyrus Tobin called.

OCTOBER 2.   I wrote a letter to one of my Nova Scotia best friends, Mabel Sproul.

OCTOBER 10.   Willie went to the orchard and picked 5 bushels of McIntosh apples. They make the nicest red sauce.

DECEMBER 9.   Willie found a little crippled bird and brought it home. We have put it in a box to feed it.

1967

JANUARY 29.   We didn't get home from Grange until 12:00 P.M., and there was so much to talk about. We were honored for our 60 year membership.

MARCH 10.   Willie is still making chairs down cellar, and at the shop. He has made a nice sled for Pamela, and painted it red.

MAY 5.   Willie washed the floors for me.

JUNE 7.   The apple blossoms are out and pretty, and the leaves are coming out very fast.

JULY 20.   Dr. Giddings seems to think I am doing pretty well, for my age. Mended for Willie. I did a very large ironing and I was so proud to get it done. Cyrus Tobin calls every day.

SEPTEMBER 20. Just did general work. When Willie is out, I am very lonesome. When he comes in, I sit beside him, and once I said, "I hate to go and leave you."

[The diary of so many years ended at this time. Her health continued to fail, and her mind became troubled and wandering. The days of pain seemed to have passed, and she died October 14, 1968. She had a happy disposition. She was pleased with very little. I made the original abstract from the diary and then, to fit the scheme of the book, this number had to be cut by at least half. — Will Penney]

Dorothy Penney's Young Life

Dorothy Penney was born in Belgrade, January 6, 1912.

Her great aunt, Eliza Penney Rollins, taught her to read at home, and she was able to skip the first grade on entering school at the age of six. At first her mother went with her a few times to meet the school wagon, as it seemed a long ways for one so small and timid to go alone and there were strange noises in the woods. It took all of her courage to pass a place where a big woodchuck lived.

She was a slender, brown-eyed girl, quiet and thoughtful for her age, and not at all given to "spreading the news," as some children are.

Her mother said that she could not recall once in her school life when Dorothy had to be called in the morning. She very seldom missed school because of sickness. Once she lost a few days because of a throat operation. Her first words on coming out from under the ether were, "Oh, Mama, am I really alive?" "Yes, didn't you expect to be?" "No."

Until she reached the 8th grade, she went to the one-room school that once stood on the east side of the Bog Road. Her teacher, Arabina Twombley, once said of her, "If they were all like Dorothy, I would like to teach. She always knows her lessons, and never makes any trouble." Her rank was such that she was usually excused from examinations. Beyond the 7th grade, she went to the Central School at Belgrade Depot. At this time she started taking music and drawing lessons. In 1926 she started a diary and maintained it with few breaks until she entered the hospital in 1940. It is written in a happy vein about her work and every-day events. She frequently noted the day's weather and the fact that she had "studied hard."

When the first 4-H club was organized in Belgrade, she was elected its first president. She won a county championship in sewing and was awarded a free trip to the Springfield Exposition in 1929. That summer she spent several weeks visiting relatives in Massachusetts and Connecticut. In the fall of that year she entered Bates College, majoring in English. She took a leading part in many college activities, being manager of the soccer and hockey teams and a member of a number of clubs and committees. We think she enjoyed her college life a great deal, but she never

The young contemporaries of Dorothy Penney: Belgrade High School in 1926.

Left to right: Front row: Calvin Wentworth, William Rix, Harry French, Chester Sawyer, Laurence Brawn, Donald Mosher, Richard Sturtevant, Walter Woodbury, Walter Johnson, Joseph Kinney. Second row: Ervin Farnham, Ray Sawyer, Olive Pray, Dorothy Guptill, Edythe Gleason, Lurline Alexander, Beulah Brooks, Natalie Taylor, Mrs. John S. Carver (assistant teacher), Syrena Cook, Robert B. Dow (principal). Third row: Ernest Cook, Vernal Furbush, Raymond Freeman, Earl Higgins, Leslie Brown, William Damren, Vera Dalton, Louise Littlefield, Dorothy Penney, Beatrice Damren. Fourth row: Dennis Bickford, Phyllis Brooks, Mildred French, Annie Pray, Christine Cook, Viola Gray, Mildred Stevens.

spoke of it as college but as just "going to school." A part of the time at Bates she waited on tables to help out on her expenses. Once when she had earned ten dollars in this way, she was paid with a new bill. On reaching her room she discovered a second bill adhering to the first one. She promptly carried one back.

Weak arches gave her some foot trouble, but she did this table-waiting work for five summers, mostly at Monhegan Island— and at Ogunquit. The pay was small and the tips also—in those depression times. But a lady once rewarded her with twenty-five dollars. At another time an old gentleman of Semitic descent on leaving the table said, "Miss Penney there is a fly in the sugar bowl. Please attend to it at once." A hurried investigation revealed a ten dollar bill tucked in the bowl.

The year following graduation from Bates in 1933 was mostly spent at home on the farm. She had never lost interest in her early drawing lessons. During this year she commenced a corresponding art course. She devoted a good deal of time to this with the hope of sometime becoming a commercial artist. She never quite finished the course. She also kept reviewing her school books, "to keep brushed up," as she said. And during this year she did a little substituting in the Belgrade High School from which she had graduated such a short time before.

In the fall of 1934 she commenced teaching French and English in the high school at Washburn in Aroostook County. Here she first met Kenneth Mansfield. His family once lived at Jonesport, where they had a large store. He was a graduate of Colby in the class of 1931. He had gone to Washburn three years before to teach history and coach basketball. He had unusual success in developing winning ball teams, and he was respected and appreciated by the boys.

Dorothy taught at Washburn for two years, and on vacations they often came back to the farm together.

In the fall of 1936 Kenneth started teaching in Ellsworth and Dorothy in Belgrade High School, making it possible for her to live at home. In spite of the distance that separated them, they saw each other quite often and commenced to think seriously of marriage. Before making this decision, Dorothy anxiously consulted her mother, saying, "It is awful hard to leave this dear, quiet place. It is such a good home."

Standing before the south bay window in her home, they were married on June 6, 1937. After a wedding trip to Canada and Niagara Falls, they started keeping house at 35 Rodick Street, Bar Harbor, where Kenneth was to teach in the high school and coach basketball.

Their married life was very happy, and they soon made many friends in Bar Harbor. They both joined the Congregational Church and several clubs. Dorothy became an active worker in all Y.W.C.A. efforts, and a frequent speaker on literary subjects. She lived a very active and fruitful life at this time, taking part in club programs, coaching plays, substituting in the high school, helping Kenneth with his school papers, and acting as one of the advisers for the Girl Reserves.

Summer at Bar Harbor was a busy time, and they both worked in the community. Kenneth ran the Information Bureau at the dock and Dorothy waited on tables at a hotel during her first summer. Here she sometimes heard the work of her husband praised by visiting tourists who were not aware they had such an interested listener. One day some new guests were discussing their good fortune in having secured his services as a guide for a tour of Mt. Desert Island. One of them said to her, "Do you happen to know that nice young man at the dock?" "Yes. He is my husband."

Her last two summers in Bar Harbor, she was employed in a dress shop operated by Mrs. Goodrich. Already experienced in sewing, she became a good dressmaker.

Helping to set up in housekeeping, her art course, and other things called for quite a lot of money, and she was rather free in making presents, but she was able to save five hundred dollars by October, 1940.

Early in September of this last year, Kenneth and Dorothy attended the World's Fair in New York, making a short visit at home on the way back to Bar Harbor. She reported to us that the summer had been too busy for her to do anything on the "History of the Penney Family," which she had commenced. They had a fine time at the Fair, but for her perhaps the happiest part was to describe the wonderful things she had seen to us stay-at-homes. She was a good story-teller who loved to entertain, and she took us to the Fair with her imagination.

They planned to visit at home again during the first week of October, but the second night before starting she was taken sick and had to go immediately to the hospital. Her last well day had been very happily spent on a five mile hike over Mt. Desert Island with her landlord's wife, Mrs. Carter.

The cause of her sickness, a ruptured appendix, was not well understood at the Bar Harbor Hospital, and the doctor did not operate at first, a great mistake. Intravenous feeding was resorted to and a tube placed through one nostril to keep the stomach quieted. She became nostalgic saying, "More than anything in this world, I wish my mother could come." It happened that her mother was just out of the Augusta Hospital and was unable to got to Bar Harbor for a period. But she wrote Dorothy a letter every day and called often by telephone. Kenneth was with her constantly and saw that everything possible was done.

An operation was finally performed after she had been weeks in the hospital, but it could give only temporary relief. As un-

Kenneth and Dorothy Penney Mansfield at the farm about 1939.

favorable symptoms developed, she kept them to herself as long as she could, saying, "I don't want anyone to worry."

When at last her mother entered the sick room, Dorothy stretched out her hands towards her saying, "Oh, Mum, it is so good of you to come. The operation is over, and I am better, lots better. I'll soon be able to go home."

But her mother, overcome at seeing her so changed, could not remember that she was able to say a word during the minute or so she was allowed to stay in the room. The nurses reported to her that "In all of Dorothy's sickness there has never been one word of complaint at her hard lot, but only gratitude for the care and the flowers. She is the nicest patient we have had since the hospital was built. We want her to live as much as you do."

We saw her once more two days later, and she was not so well.

It was so hard for us to realize that she could be so changed. Her face was anxious and distressed. Her decline of the recent past she realized, although she would not admit it. Perhaps she wanted to hide what the future might hold as long as she could, as she waved us away with her one free hand saying, "I'm alright, I'm alright. Don't worry."

She died the next day, just before noon. We were not there, but they said the end was like the coming of sleep. We were reached in her little rooms above the paint store with the sad news. We could only leave for home.

November 1, the day of the funeral, was one of the brightest and fairest of the fall. George went to the Belgrade Depot Express office for the flowers shipped from Bar Harbor and found so many that he had to come back to the farm for a truck. Dorothy was back in the house where she had been born and on the spot before the big bay window where she had been married three years before. The funeral sermon was delivered by the minister who had performed the marriage.

As the entrance to the Penney farm road is rather blind coming off the county road, a special sign was put up with the words, "Penney Road. Mansfield Funeral." Mrs. Goodrich, her Bar Harbor employer, had left Maine for the season to go to her home in Augusta, Georgia. On hearing of what had happened, she came

112

back for the funeral. Many friends came from Bar Harbor, and seven from her Bates College class. The lower part of the house was filled and part of the above. The fifty-four cards with the flowers bore the names of 256 people. While examining these, Kenneth said, "I never could have accomplished half what I have in Bar Harbor without the many helpful contacts she made. Everybody loved her, and when she went to the hospital, I had to give up going anywhere on foot, so many people stopped me to inquire about Dorothy."

The very large attendance at the funeral and the many flowers made us think she was perhaps better known and appreciated by others than by ourselves.

In regarding some aspects of Dorothy's childhood and her later life, I recalled a certain quotation: "There is a destiny that shapes our ends, rough-hew them as we may." And I am aware that scientists would say "oldwives tales" at what I am about to write. But it may be that the personality of the child is deeply influenced by the attitude of the mother while the child is in the womb. In our family we had these two great contrasts.

My father was a large and powerful man who always enjoyed the best of health and could read without glasses to the end of his days. But he did not have a good disposition. This tended to make his life unhappy, and it was hard for those who had to live with him. He was not improved by the many troubles and worriments that fell as his lot.

His sister, Eliza Penney Rollins (1845-1944), once remarked about Father: "There was a space of five years between him and his older brother, Martin, and when Mother knew that she was going to have another child, she was mad, and she didn't become reconciled during the whole period." And when Father was born in 1852, it was soon found that he was not an easy baby to take care of. Aunt Eliza, who had a very clear memory of these times, said, "He cried, until he was old enough to be good and ugly." We are sorry for the hard life that was his lot.

Dorothy's mother had a good disposition and probably the happiest time in her life was while she was expecting her first baby. She was careful to be cheerful and agreeable at all times, thinking it might make a difference. When this first baby was

113

born, it was soon found to be a very nice one, easily cared for and hardly ever causing any trouble. She seldom cried, and it was never necessary to punish her or say "no" more than once.

After Dorothy had learned to play a bit, an old lady of the neighborhood, Octavia Weeks, who used to walk by the house, called to see the new baby. She would take the playthings away from Dorothy for a minute, and then give them back, then take them away again. She explained that she was testing her temper and disposition. She finally pronounced it, after these experiments, one of the best. So it proved, for she was so obedient, so thoughtful and considerate that she missed many of the adventures and accidents that befall some children. The happy, smiling disposition that was hers lasted until the very end, and helped to bind the many friendships that she made.

It was her way to think of others first and be as kind and helpful as she could be. No matter how trying the situation was, she never became impatient or did a mean or selfish act.

Her mother was her dearest friend and companion. She always consulted her, and they were together as much as possible. If it happened that her mother didn't approve of some trip, she would say, "Alright, Mama, I won't go." She never learned to operate a car, but her mother was a good driver and together they went in the Model T to Grange and school programs. At these school parties she learned to dance so well that she sometimes gave exhibitions as a helper at local events.

At home she had no playmates of her own age, so she depended on herself for amusement. She was easily entertained. She thought it was wrong to be a cause of trouble, and she took care not to offend in any way. She seldom asked for anything. But it was a pleasure to do things for her, she was so grateful and appreciative. Her willingness to help was limited only by her strength.

It was no doubt a very fine thing for her that she taught regularly for several years and continued as a substitute teacher after her marriage. In this way she met many young people and, in some degree, influenced their lives at a time when they were being molded for the future. She always managed also to devote a good deal of time to projects outside of her work. All of this

114

was a good thing for her, as it enabled her to outgrow a shyness in meeting strangers that had troubled her some as a child. She gradually acquired a grace and ease of manner through these experiences that helped make her welcome everywhere.

Our people cleared most of the original part of this farm and adding to it little by little, have lived on it continuously since 1817. Dorothy was of the fifth generation of Belgrade Penneys. She thought this was a remarkable record, as indeed it is when so few families live in the same place for even one generation.

With her rural background Dorothy acquired a love for nature and a nostalgic longing for the life that the country gives that we, who are still in the old ways, may never know. She always loved to "explore" the fields and woods. When she found herself living in town, she would take long walks in the country.

There is a pretty pine grove on the shore of Belgrade Stream, where the bank is steep, that she loved the best of all. She went here many times for a picnic or to spend time in the shade. In her short life she lived in a number of different places sometimes in beautiful surroundings, but her love seemed to grow for her first home. Any new improvement or convenience installed on the farm made her the happiest of all. Once in that last year, she confessed to her brother, George: "I always dread going away. I love the sounds of the farm, the hens and the cattle."

Landscape on the north side of the Penney farm bordering Belgrade Stream.

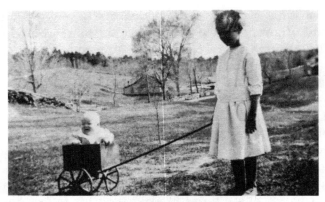

Dorothy Penney wheeling George on the farm, 1920.

Sometimes she would take a little walk and look again at the fields and buildings. It is perhaps possible that those who till this farm in the future, and enjoy its many conveniences, will contemplate the great tasks performed here to make this farm and will love the place as did Dorothy whose presence and contribution was such a shining example of bravery and surpassing goodness.

She always went to church and Sunday School where she sometimes taught a class. In school her passionate fondness for poetry was known to her classmates who used to remark, "Has Dot judged this poem yet?" Tennyson and Wordsworth seemed to have been her favorites for there are many page corners and pencil marks marking their poems in her books which she liked best.

Her study and teaching of literature encouraged her taste for good reading which she pursued as much as she could. Books that described difficult situations on the uphill road with the end sometimes shrouded in sadness, appealed to her most. She liked *A Tale of Two Cities, Lorna Doone, The Garden of Allah, Green Mansions, Kamongo, Gone With the Wind, John Brown's Body,* all classics of their kind.

Vacation time for Dorothy meant merely a change of work. Weighing 104 pounds, she was never sick until the last, except for a cold. With this constant employment, she was not able to pursue her art studies as she would like to have done. She thought this held some of her brightest hopes. She was about at the end of

116

the course she had started years before. In one of her art books she had read: "A little genius with a whale of an appetite for work, and things are bound to turn out right." She had underlined this, with a note, "Wonderful," in a bold hand. Time did not allow her dream to be realized.

She was not conceited in the least, rather the reverse, underrating her abilities more than she should. Trials and disappointments that come to all she never mentioned, even in her diary, which contains no thought of bitterness.

Dorothy was always hesitant, almost apologetic, in asking for help, and she would even at times change her mind and get along without it. Once her mother told me that Dorothy needed ten dollars for something. I left it at the house for her and went on about my business for the day. After she had gone, I found the bill in the pocket of my best pants.

In the spring of that last year, we visited her for a day in Bar Harbor. It was the 18th of May and spring was at its height. She was so happy showing us the Island places that when we walked about she was often a step or two ahead. Her diary tells about this visit and the entry ends with the words: "They are gone, and it's pretty lonesome."

Benjamin Franklin once said, "I will speak ill of no man." Dorothy was a strict observer of this rule, and her sympathy for others made their misfortunes touch her almost as her own. She made friends easily and had very many. Her personality was always the same, and her greetings carried the tone of real friendliness.

Her self control was such that she never showed anger. After she grew up she was only once seen in tears. That was the occasion of the burning of the new Washburn High School, where she had just commenced teaching. She was able to meet unexpected conditions with calm and ability. Her husband said, "I was always proud of her."

When sickness and suffering finally came, she bore it with such patience that the nurses said, "She is the nicest patient we have ever had." As in happier days, her concern was still for others, and it worried her to think that she was causing so much trouble. Although she failed constantly, we fully expected her to

117

recover, she was so young, so cheerful, and had always been so gay and full of life. Now we think she realized how serious her condition was. Towards the last she did not seem to want us where we would see her suffer and sent us a message, "Not to work so hard." Her last words to us were, "I'm alright, I'm alright. Don't worry."

While her thoughts were busy with concern for others,

> "Her soul to Him who gave it rose,
> God lead it to its long repose,
> Its glorious rest!
> And, though her earthly sun has set,
> Its light shall linger round us yet,
> Bright, radiant, blest."*

and

> "To live in hearts we leave behind is not to die."

She lives and has a bright place in our memory. Perhaps she is here now and in the far places where she lived, in the sun, the wind and the rain, and in the green leaves.

Most of our people have lived long and useful lives. One, Hannay Penney Littlefield (1761-1868), attained the great age of 106 years and six months. Dorothy did not go until her pleasing personality and unusual worth was recognized by all who knew her. How much we miss her thin, eager face and gentle ways, always so anxious to please, and expecting so little for herself. But perhaps she lived the best part of life without having to know what it is like to be feeble and old. She is one of the "Old Penneys" now that she always liked to inquire about.

On the first leaf of a new diary volume that she started during her second year at Bates, I found the following verse:

> "I have to live with myself and so,
> I want to be fit for myself to know;
> I want to be able, as days go by,
> Always to look myself straight in the eye.
> I don't want to stand with the setting sun,
> And hate myself for the things I've done.
> I want to go out with my head erect,

*Paraphrase of a verse by Coplas de Manrique, translated by Longfellow.

118

I want to deserve all men's respect,
And here in the struggle for fame and pelf,
I want to be able to like myself.
I don't want to look at myself and know
That I'm bluster, bluff, and idle show.
I never can hide myself from me.
I see what others may never see,
I know what others may never know,
I never can fool myself and so
Whatever happens I want to be
Self-respecting and conscience-free."

When I first made these biographical notes thirty years ago, I felt certain reservations about the task because of Dorothy's opinion that could not be expressed. But I went ahead feeling

Dorothy Penney about 1938.

119

that the example of so good a life and one that deserves so much to be remembered should not be lost.

As a token of love, the 1941 yearbook of Bar Harbor High School was dedicated to Dorothy and carried her picture.

Perhaps when we have grown old and life has become a burden not worth living, we may be able to go as cheerfully as Dorothy, who was leaving so much.

Will Penney in his retirement.

Penney Furrows in the Maine Land

EXODUS FROM WELLS

In the last years of the eighteenth century several Penney families of Wells trekked from that early American town to the frontier of Belgrade and West Pond Plantation, later Dearborn, and after 1840, North Belgrade. John and Pelatiah Penney of West Pond Plantation were probably brothers of George Penney of Lot 98 adjoining Long Pond.

The following families establish the genealogical tree from George in a straight line to the present on the Penney farm in South Belgrade.

GEORGE PENNEY* Born Wells 1755. Died Belgrade, March 27, 1814. Married Abigail Wormwood, August 3, 1782, in Wells. Married Abigail Littlefield of Wells in Belgrade, January 23, 1805. (Abigail Littlefield Penney was living in Wells in 1835).

Children:

John Penney, born May 3, 1786. Died Belgrade, March 20, 1872.

Christiana Penney, born May 12, 1788.

Betsey Penney, born April 14, 1790.

Joshua Penney, born June 6, 1796. Died January 21, 1799.

Abigail Penney, born June 26, 1798.

James Penney, born October 3, 1801. Died November 11, 1801.

Lucy, born November 1, 1802.

Mehitabel Penney, born January 6, 1806.

Patience Penney, born April 14, 1808.

*George Penney's father and mother were Thomas Penney, Jr., and Adah Hatch Spear Penney, widow of Gideon Spear. Thomas Penney, probably the father of Thomas, Jr., was listed as an inhabitant of Wells in 1726.

JOHN PENNEY (of Belgrade) born Wells, May 3, 1786. Died Belgrade, March 20, 1872. Married Betsey Taylor of Readfield, May 7, 1809.

Children:

Abigail, born December 23, 1809. Died November 17, 1825.

Knowlton Penney, born September 15, 1810.

Betsey Penney, born March 11, 1812.

Martha Penney, born August 6, 1814.

John W. Penney, born October 14, 1819. Died March 8, 1892.

George Johnson Penney, born January 16, 1828.

(JOHN PENNEY also married Mary Mitchell. Died December 24, 1879).

JOHN W. PENNEY Born October 14, 1819. Died March 8, 1892. Married Hannah M. Williams. Born October 31, 1824. Died June 23, 1914.

Children:

Eliza Ellen Penney, born September 15, 1845. Died January 11, 1944.

Martin Luther Penney, born August 13, 1847. Died July 26, 1918.

John Newton Penney, born September 7, 1852. Died May 13, 1939.

Laura Ella Penney, born May 7, 1855. Died July 27, 1944.

Justin B. Penney, born September 8, 1858. Died October 26, 1934.

George A. Penney, born June 6, 1861. Died October 19, 1943.

JOHN NEWTON PENNEY Born September 7, 1852. Died May 13, 1939. Married Celia E. White of Fort Fairfield. Born September 20, 1859. Died August 30, 1937.

Children:

John William Penney, born October 16, 1882.

Eva Penney, born November 8, 1883. Died March 13, 1947.

Harry Penney, born February 10, 1885. Died March 19, 1963.

Justin Penney, born August 4, 1888. Died October 19, 1938.

Jessie Penney, born June 4, 1891.

JOHN WILLIAM PENNEY   Born October 16, 1882. Married
   Minnie Mills Penney of Sidney on July 21, 1909.
   Children:
   Dorothy Penney, born January 6, 1912. Died October 30,
      1940.
   George Lendall Penney, born September 28, 1919.

Early Jones & Prescott 1795 Plan of Belgrade Showing George Penney's Lot 98

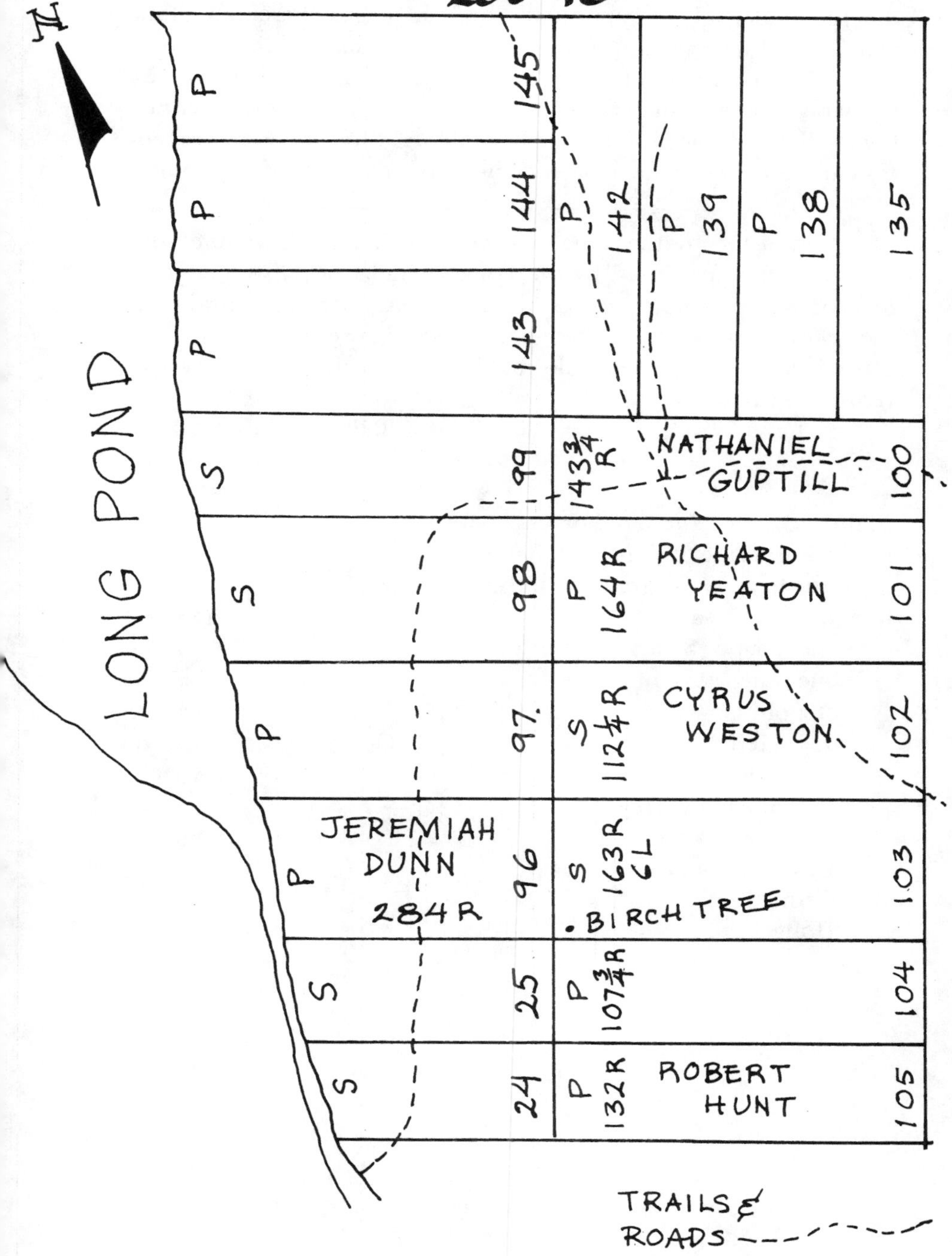
N
LONG POND
145
144
143
99
98
97
96
25
24
142
139
138
135
143¾ R
NATHANIEL GUPTILL
100
164 R
RICHARD YEATON
101
112¼ R
CYRUS WESTON
102
JEREMIAH DUNN
284 R
163 R
6 L
BIRCH TREE
103
107¾ R
104
132 R
ROBERT HUNT
105
P
S
TRAILS & ROADS

INVENTORY OF PROPERTY OF GEORGE PENNEY

When George Penney of Lot 98 died in Belgrade in 1814, the Judge of Probate appointed Abraham Page, Sherebiah Clark and James Lumbard appraisers to inventory and value the property of the deceased. It should be borne in mind that the list probably does not include all of the items in the George Penney house. Some things would have been thought too valueless to mention and others may have been claimed by members of the family.

"Agreeable to the warrant hereunto annexed we the subscribers being appointed by the Hon. Daniel Cony Esq. Judge of Probate for the County of Kennebec a Committee to appraise all the real and personal Estate whereof George Penney late of Belgrade Deceased died seized do make the following Inventory and return, to wit:

Belgrade July 1st, 1814

	Dols	Cts
Eighty acres of Land more or less laying on the south side of the North half of Lott 98 in the town of Belgrade with the Buildings thereon. Valued	400	00
one yoke of Stears	30	00
one other yoke of Stears	25	00
one old Cow	12	00
one Heifer	12	00
one Horse	10	00
one Shoat or Hog	2	00
nine Sheep and six Lambs	20	00
Ring and Staple		34
Grind Stone	1	00
Dung Fork		50

Slay	5	00
one Hay Fork		17
Ring and Staple		17
seven Harrow Teeth	2	00
one Adze		25
Hay Fork		25
Round Table		50
one Chest		50
one Feather Bed Bolster two Pillows	4	00
two Sheets	1	00
one green Bedquilt	2	50
three old Sheets		75
Bedstead and Cord		60
Table Cloth		50
one other Bedstead and Cord		50
one Slaie No. 30 at Ell		33
Book Town Officer		25
one pair Pillow Cases		25
one under Bed		50
two old Quilts		50
Chest of Draws	1	50
Loom	1	00
Crane and Hooks	1	00
one Pail Pot		75
one Tea Kettle		50
two old Scythes		25
one Scythe and Irons for two	1	00
two Sickles		50
Spoon Mould		50
Looking Glass		75
10 lb. old Pewter		80
Bridle .50 Saddle 1.50	2	00
two barrels		50
one Swarm of Bees	6	00
one Axe .50 Seven Dollars Cash 7.00	7	50

557.91

Abraham Page
Sherebiah Clark — Committee
James Lumbard

An analysis of this inventory reveals something of the way of life of George Penney the Belgrade pioneer. Certain logical items are missing from the inventory, the yokes for the "stears" and most of the kitchen utensils that must have been on the property. The list is easily read in the original except for two words, the one that seems to be "Adze" and the word following "Loom."

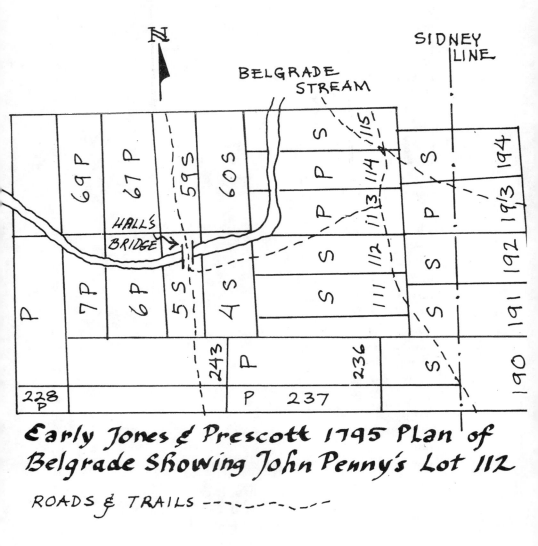

Early Jones & Prescott 1795 Plan of Belgrade Showing John Penny's Lot 112

ROADS & TRAILS ---- ---- ---- --

THE PENNEYS OF WEST POND PLANTATION

As these Penneys were so closely related to our own direct ancestor, George Penney, and made up a part of the migration from Wells to this region at the same time about 1800, we make this notice of what we know about these early Penneys in what is now North Belgrade.

The Kennebec Proprietors, in accordance with their title from Plymouth Colony before the Revolution, owned originally all of these Belgrade lands. For a time after 1750 they were very active in surveying and developing their property below Augusta. But as they were largely a Loyalist group at the time of the Revolution, they were obliged to abandon their activities and interests here for many years. For a time after the Revolution they were socially and politically not acceptable in these parts. It was during this time that large numbers of "squatters" came onto their lands. And when the young heirs of the Proprietors commenced to reassert their interest and rights here after 1800, they found, over wide areas of their property, squatters in physical possession, many of them Revolutionary soldiers, the very rabble in arms that had forced the Loyalists out of the country in the 1775-1783 period.

It seems fairly plain that the Penneys of West Pond Plantation were a part of this frontier squatter class. We know that John Penney of "West Pond Settlement," for a sum of $48.00, was "quieted in possession of 'lot No. 15' containing one hundred acres as by the plan and description of John Crosby in the office of this propriety." This indicates that John Penney had actually taken possession at some previous date and for a small payment was allowed to remain in possession of the company land. And several other Penneys were active at this time in West Pond Plantation between the north end of Salmon Lake and the south slope of Bickford Hill.

129

Other than what has been noted in the genealogical lists local records indicate that in July, 1797, Samuel Avery and Dorothea Penney, "Both of West Ponds," were married; that in November, 1801, Benjamin Bickford and Sally Penney "of West Ponds" were married; that in November, 1804, William Varney and Hannah Penney were married, "Both of West Ponds."

Several Penney families continued to live in the area north of Salmon Lake down to the time of the Civil War. Twenty years later, in 1879, they were all gone by that name except Manley Penney, who owned a property near the top of Bickford Hill. He seems to have been the last of the North Belgrade Penneys. These families, with the great changes that came over the country in the middle of the last century, had moved to other towns or to some other part of the nation.

And there is another explanation for the disappearance of the North Belgrade Penneys, so that to this day very few of that name are to be found in this part of the State. Joseph M. Penney of the 7th Maine Regiment of Volunteers, William W. Penney of the 15th Maine, Peletiah Penney of the 3rd Maine, and Ira D. Penney of the 31st Maine, all enlisted from Waterville, all died in the service in the holocaust of the Civil War at various points from Waterville to New Orleans. It is likely that they were all scions of the North Belgrade branch that seem to disappear about this time so abruptly and so mysteriously.

The following families were some of the pioneer Penneys of West Pond Plantation.

JOHN PENNEY (of Wells and West Pond Plantation). Born November 17, 1754. Married Sarah, born November 24, 1751.

Children:
Dolly Penney, born May 31, 1778. Died May 6, 1803.
Nehemiah Penney, born December 6, 1779.
Sarah Penney, born November 27, 1781. Died November 16, 1804.
Hannah Penney, born December 6, 1785.
John Penney, Jr., born February 17, 1787.
Susanna Penney, born March 28, 1791.
Daniel Penney, born December 2, 1792.

Lucy Penney, born June 6, 1794.

(Mark of JOHN PENNEY'S sheep, a crop off the right ear and a split in the same).

NEHEMIAH PENNEY   Born December 6, 1779. Married Elizabeth Richardson of Belgrade (born June 11, 1784) on Sunday, April 26, 1801.

Children:
Joel Penney, born August 9, 1801. Died June 7, 1802.
George Penney, born April 7, 1803.
Charles Penney, born April 19, 1805.
Greenwood Penney, born April 23, 1807.
Urial Penney, born June 16, 1809.
Nehemiah Penney, born July 15, 1811.
John Penney, born February 25, 1814.
Sarah Penney, born April 21, 1816.
Eliza Penney, born March 11, 1819.
Milton Richardson Penney, born May 5, 1820.
Silas Richardson Penney, born December 16, 1822.
Stephen P. Penney, born October 24, 1825.

JOHN PENNEY, JR.   Born February 17, 1787. Married Miss Susannah Page of Belgrade, on April 22, 1810.
Children:

Hannah Penney, born August 9, 1810.
Betsey Penney, born August 25, 1812. Died June 7, 181 (?)
Elijah Penney, born July 8, 1815.
Ezra Jonson Penney, born July 25, 1817.
Elisa Branch Penney, born June 2, 1819.
Willard Penney, born March 20, 1827.

GEORGE PENNEY (son of Nehemiah of West Pond). Born April 7, 1803.

Children:
Rozina Penney, born August 9, 1822.
Alamander Bickford Penney, born December 28, 1823.
Alpheus Lowell Penney, born March 11, 1826.
Urial R. Penney, born March 16, 1828.

Charles H. Penney, born June 28, 1830.
Malinda Penney, born September 28, 1832.
(Sheep mark registered July 9, 1829).

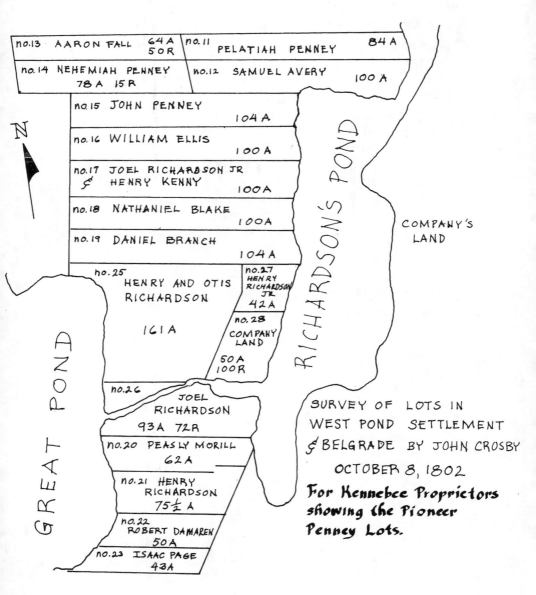

no.13 AARON FALL 64 A 50 R

no. 11 PELATIAH PENNEY 84 A

no. 14 NEHEMIAH PENNEY 78 A 15 R

no.12 SAMUEL AVERY 100 A

no. 15 JOHN PENNEY 104 A

no. 16 WILLIAM ELLIS 100 A

no. 17 JOEL RICHARDSON JR & HENRY KENNY 100 A

no. 18 NATHANIEL BLAKE 100 A

no. 19 DANIEL BRANCH 104 A

no. 25 HENRY AND OTIS RICHARDSON 161 A

no. 27 HENRY RICHARDSON JR 42 A

no. 28 COMPANY LAND 50 A 100 R

no. 26 JOEL RICHARDSON 93 A 72 R

no. 20 PEASLY MORILL 62 A

no. 21 HENRY RICHARDSON 75½ A

no. 22 ROBERT DAMAREN 50 A

no. 23 ISAAC PAGE 43 A

RICHARDSON'S POND

COMPANY'S LAND

GREAT POND

N

SURVEY OF LOTS IN WEST POND SETTLEMENT & BELGRADE BY JOHN CROSBY OCTOBER 8, 1802 For Kennebec Proprietors showing the Pioneer Penney Lots.

132

HOW THE OLD TOWN SCHOOL
DISTRICTS WERE GOVERNED

When I first started going to school over eighty years ago, the town was divided into numerous community school districts each governing itself with very little interference from the town at large. This was the common unchanged custom since the beginning of the town in 1796. When the town school districts were terminated by the State Legislature in 1893, my father was district clerk. The last school district record book was in his hands at that time and it has been preserved here on the farm.

My father, J. Newton Penney, my grandfather John W. Penney, my great grandfather John Penney, and my great-great-grandfather, Elias Taylor, are all mentioned many times in the minutes of the district meeting recorded in this book from 1834 to 1893. They provided services and held offices in the school district.

These are the minutes of the meeting for June 2, 1834:*

Met in school Meeting
1. by vote made choice of Asa Axtell moderator
2. by vote made choice of Asa Axtell Sr. clark
3. by vote made choice of John Wellman to settle with Joseph Knowles
4. voted to have eight weaks woman school
5. voted to have the school begin the first of August
6. voted to let the board at the lowest bidder board by John Wellman 60 cts a weak
7. voted the Agent buy a book to list the Districts records on
   Minutes of a meeting for September 22, 1834:
2. voted not to have any more summer schools
3. voted to set up a winter school, to begin the middle of November

---

*These record abstracts are in the original spelling and style.

4. voted to set up the wood and board at the lowest bidder
    board by Elias Taylor Sr. at one dollar a weak
    wood by Asa Axtell Sr. for 70 cents a cord

   On June 20, 1835:
3. voted to set up a womans school
4. settled with the agent and found dew the district—1.69
5. voted to have six weaks womans school
6. voted to have it begin the first monday in September
7. voted set up the board at the lowest bidder
    Elias Taylor Sr. for five shillings a weak
8. voted that Joseph Knowles pay all the money now dew and
    this years money by the first of march next, or he is out
    of the district
9. voted to chuse a committy of too to let Knowles know the
    proceedings of the district

   On September 6, 1836:
4. voted to have a Franklin stove

   In 1839:
2. voted to adjourn this meeting till next saturday at early
    candleliting

   On September 26, 1846, John W. Penney was clerk of the
meeting and he recorded:
10. voted to have no Schollars admitted from Other Districts
    With Out paying 12½ cts a Week

   On January 1, 1848:
2. voted to raise 120 dollars in tax
3. to set up the collectorship to lowest bidder and he be Treas-
    urer At one half per ct
4. William Axtell colector and treasurer
    Sold the job to Orren Rowe Sidney for one hundred and
    seven dollars

   October 29, 1850:
2. Agreeable to set up a winter school
3. To have it commence on the first of December
4. the school during the Winter to be kept by a Mistress
5. the board to the lowest bidder

6. Board by N. A. Hall $1.27 cts per week
7. the wood to be Dry hard wood and well split Maple or Beach or Birch Suitable for the Stove
8. Wood by John Wellman at $2.00 per Cord
9. A. Chamberlain survey the wood
10. Voted not to have any Scholars admited from other Districts under the Sum of 10 cts per week in advance to the agent
11. Agreed to have the Door fixt for 30 cts by J. W. Penney

April 30, 1852:
2. J. W. Penney Clerk
3. to have a Summer School
4. the School to Commence on the 2nd Monday in May
7. to have one third of the Money laid out in a Summer School

The last minutes are for April 4, 1893, and they were kept by my father:

Met in School meeting According to warrent
1. T. E. Penney Moderator
2. J. N. Penney Clerk
3. Wm. H. Knowles Agent
4. Summer School to commence the first Monday in May
5. the fall School to commence the first Monday in September
6. Voted to have a female teacher
7. Board by J. N. Penney at $2.00
8. a the wood J. N. Penney for 6.00
9. the repares by the Agent
10. Disolved Said Meeting

> J. N. Penney
> Dis No 4
> District Clerk

For many years in the last century Titcomb Academy operated on the south pinnacle of Belgrade Hill. My Uncle Mandeville Rollins (1837-1914), who married Aunt Eliza in 1867, was a student in the Academy in 1854 with George Minot, C. Marshall Weston, Henry F. D. Wyman and other memorable local persons of the century.

135

TEXT-BOOKS.

LATIN.

Weld's Latin Lessons; Andrews and Stoddard's Latin Grammar; Cicero's Orations; Anthon's Sallust; Cooper's Virgil; Leverett's Latin Lexicon.

GREEK.

Arnold's Greek Lessons; Sophocles' Greek Grammar; Jacob's Greek Reader; Liddell and Scott's Greek-English Lexicon.

FRENCH.

Pinney's Exercises; Ollendorff's Grammar; Modern French Reader, (Rowan's); Callot's Dramatic Reader; Surenne's Dictionary.

ENGLISH.

Greenleaf's Arithmetics; Mitchell's Primary Geography; Pelton's Outline Maps; Mitchell's Ancient Geography; Worcester's History; Weld's Grammar; Cutler's Physiology; Comstock's Philosophy; Johnston's Farmer's Chemistry; Smyth's Algebras; Davis' Legendre; Davies' Surveying.

LOCATION

This institution is pleasantly situated, in the northern part of Belgrade, but ten miles distant from Waterville, on the line of the Androscoggin and Kennebec Railroad, also on the stage road leading from Augusta to Anson, and is thus easy of access from all parts of the State.

BUILDINGS.

The institution has been recently repaired, and will the coming season be considerably altered.

EXPENSES.

High English and Languages,	$3 50
Common branches,	3 00
Primary Department,	2 00

Board from $1,00 to $1,50.
Books are furnished at Portland prices.

A page from the 1854 catalogue of Titcomb Academy.

AXTELL SCHOOL
Abandoned as a schoolhouse about 1900.

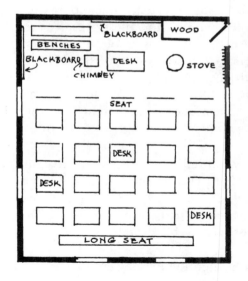

House was about 20 ft. square. Desks and seats of rock maple. In my grandmother's time it was crowded. It was adapted for a schoolhouse according to plans of Asa Axtell.

In the whole span of Belgrade school experience the highest intellectual achievement was probably reached in Titcomb Academy. This was the last Belgrade generation to read and write in the language of Socrates.

Although most of the students were from local families, some came from distant Maine towns and a few from out of State. During the term they boarded in various homes around Belgrade Hill.

The Academy building was burned down in 1885. An octogenarian who remembered the event told us in 1933 that the fire was set by a disgruntled old woman who lived on the hill. The doorstep can be found today marking the spot where the building stood.

LONGEVITY IN THE PENNEY FAMILY

It may be that longevity does run in families. That claim has been made. There seems to be some evidence to support this theory in the history of the Penney family. The most conspicuous example was Hannah Penney of Wells, a sister of the pioneer George Penney of Belgrade. Hannah was born in Wells July 16, 1761. She married Asael Littlefield, a member of that very prolific and widespread family in Wells. Records indicate that they had eight children, most of them born in Wells. In 1804 the family moved to Belgrade, apparently following other Penneys who had gone before them.

Asael and Hannah Penney Littlefield continued to live in Belgrade where Asael died in 1841. During the last years of her life Hannah lived with her daughter, Chistianna, Mrs. David Guptill, in Winslow. She died at their residence in January, 1868, at the age of 106 years, the most memorable example of longevity in the Penney family.

Hannah Littlefield visited here on the Penney farm when she was about one hundred year old. Father saw her at that time and he told us of this visit many years later.

WAGON TRAIL TO THE OLD NORTHWEST

Hannah Penney's first-born son, Samuel Littlefield, born in Wells, December 5, 1791, came to Belgrade with the family. During the War of 1812 he became a musician with one of the Belgrade militia companies. About this time he fell in love with Mary Jones, a daughter of Mary Yeaton Burks Jones and Jacob Jones, living on the West Road, and a niece of Paul (1762-1856), the pioneer Yeaton in Belgrade. Samuel and Mary became engaged.

The Yeaton-Jones family came to Belgrade in 1804 from Lebanon, the place of origin of many Belgrade pioneer families. It is legendary that during the War of 1812 one of the Jones family had been with Harrison's army in the Northwest, and his glowing stories of that country excited the spirit of adventure in the Jones family, and they decided in 1815 to migrate to the far frontier land.

Samuel, when this decision was made, had contracted to teach a summer term of school in Belgrade, so he was not able to join the main party at the time they started off in two ox-drawn covered wagons in the spring of 1815. Betsey Jones (1796-1873), a sister of Mary, was the only member of the family to remain in Belgrade. She had married John Worster. The wagon party was made up of Mary Yeaton and Jacob Jones, and the children Mary (b. 1798), Richard Yeaton Jones (1793-1873), Samuel Jones (1800-1874), Nerisa Jones (1801-1882), John Jones (1802-1833), Anna Jones (1805-1883), Experience Jones (b. 1807), and Joanna Burks, Mary's daughter by a former marriage.

The Yeaton-Jones wagons rolled slowly south and west in that summertime of 1815 for about three months until they struck a point on the Allegheny River. The wagons were sold here, a

139

flatboat was built, and they proceeded down the Allegheny and the Ohio until cold weather overtook them at Cincinnati.

Samuel, when his term of school was completed, made up a traveling kit and on horseback followed his heart west. He took the land route into Ohio and his horse died at Zanesville from the effects of the long journey. He then went to Cincinnati, arriving too late to overtake the Jones party in the spring of 1816. Here he bought a small raft and floated down the Ohio to the confluence with the Wabash and up this river to Fort Harrison on the later site of Terre Haute. The Yeaton-Jones party had left Cincinnati with the thaw. Stopping a few days at Vincennes, they had preceded Samuel and arrived before him at the Fort. After the lapse of a long year this primitive post was the scene of the reunion of the Belgrade travelers.

By glimmering candlelight, under the stolid gaze of swarthy Indians squatting in the shadows, Mary and Samuel were married by Major Chunn, Commandant of Fort Harrison, shortly following this 1816 reunion. The first child of this marriage, Thomas Littlefield, was born at the Fort in 1818 directly after Samuel and Mary had to seek its protection under threat of an Indian raid upon their settlement.

When the Yeaton-Jones wagons left Belgrade in the spring of 1815, among many other possessions, a cat was taken on board. After a lapse of about two years, in 1817, this cat reappeared in the West Road neighborhood of his old home. It was believed then, by his markings, that this was without doubt the self-same cat and that he had made the wilderness trip back from the Northwest alone to his first Belgrade home.

In April, 1837, after the trials of settlement on the Northwest frontier of a twenty year period, Mary Jones Littlefield wrote back to her stay-at-home sister, Betsey Jones Worster, in Belgrade relating what had happened in her pioneer family in recent years.

Dear and affectinate Brother and Sister.

I take this opportunity to inform you that we are all well. I hope that these few lines will find you the same.

I will inform you that our poor old mother expired on the 6th day of July 1835 was bent over with the infirmities of old age. Brother John expired on the 3rd day of March 1833 he was drowned in a little creek near his fathers. He was walking crost on a log and it was supposed that it swam around with him and no one to assist him.

There is four of us that live in this country. Richard and Samuel are doing well, Richard lives about five miles of us and has a good farm, he has five children. Samuel lives in about a half a mile has a good farm 6 children. Ann lives in about a quarter of a miles of us.

I want you to write to me. I want of my Uncles and Aunts are all living and cousins likewise. We have 2 sons and 2 daughters I want to know how you are doing and how many children you have. I live in a plentiful country. We have plenty to eat and to drink.

Corn is from twenty to thirty cents a bushel and wheat is a dollar a bushel. Cheese is twelve cents a pound. Butter is twenty cents a pound.

Me and my daughters made a hundred and eighty dollars worth of butter and cheese.

Best respects to you and your family and all inquiring friends.

Mary Littlefield to Betsey Wooster

Please to write immediately as soon as you get this letter. Direct your letters to Bloomfield Post Office Edgar Co., Illinois.

Mary Littlefield

Please give my best regards to my cousins tell them I should like to see them all.

Hannah Littlefield niece to
Aunt Betsey Worster

My youngest child is a daughter we call her Christianna after her Aunt Christianna Guptil.

Mary Littlefield*

So in this way, through Samuel Littlefield, the first son of Hannah Penney, did the Penneys of Wells and Belgrade contribute to the great American Western adventure. The descendants of Samuel and Mary are numerous in Indiana and Illinois today.

*Most of what we know about this trek comes from a descendant on the western end of the trail, Mrs. J. Floyd Gilbert of Chrisman, Illinois, a great-great-granddaughter of Samuel and Mary. The original of the letter is now in the possession of Ruth Wilkin Frazier, Paris, Illinois.

Cobbler's bench, tools — and childrens' shoes — used by John Penney (1786-1872). It is probable that he made these shoes before 1830.

Baby carriage used for Aunt Eliza before 1850. It once had a top.

Portable crib-cradle in two positions used in Aunt Eliza's (1845-1944) young life.

Combination high chair-rocking chair showing the ingenuity of the early mass producers of furniture in the nineteenth century.

146

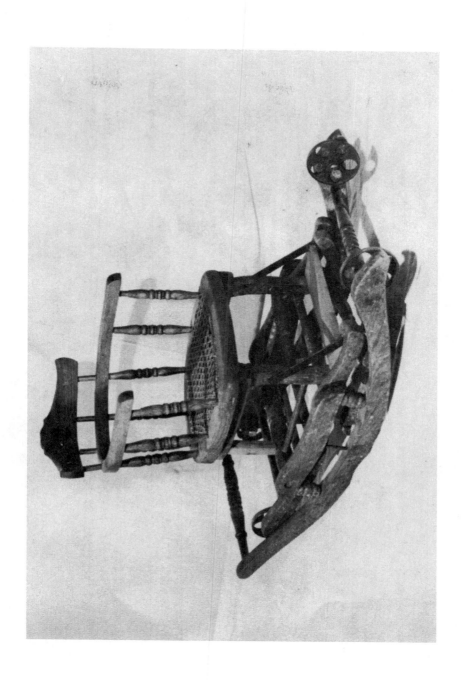

Spinning wheel used on the farm by Hannah Williams Penney (1824-1914) and Celia White Penney (1859-1937).

Vice used for repairing harnesses.

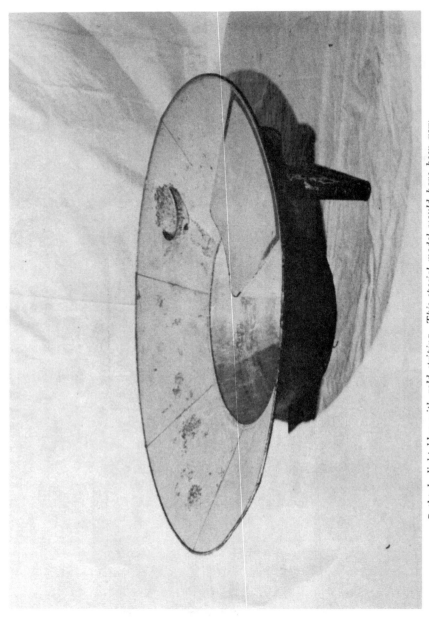

Bathtub, light blue with gold striping. This special model would have been very rarely found on Kennebec farms in the Civil War period.

SOURCE OF THE ORIGINAL PENNEY
LAND TITLES IN BELGRADE

1496　King Henry VII of England commissioned John Cabot to make discoveries in the Western Hemisphere.

1606　King James I granted the New England Charter to the Council of Plymouth.

1629　A grant was made by the Plymouth Council to the Plymouth Colony of the Kennebec Patent, with borders in the Kennebec from just below Swan Island to the mouth of the Wesserunsett Stream and fifteen miles back from the banks on each side of the river.

1648　William Bradford of Plymouth Colony bought up from the Indians their titles to the entire Kennebec valley.

1661　Plymouth Colony sold the Kennebec grant to Antipas Boyes, Edward Tyng, Thomas Brattle, and John Winslow.

1749　Descendants of the above four organized as the Kennebec Proprietors to claim their long-vacant Kennebec lands and survey, develop, and settle them.

1775　The development business of the Kennebec Proprietors was very largely broken up by the Revolutionary War and in after years squatters on their uncared for lands produced chaos in the titles.

1797　Samuel Stewart sold the north half of lot no. 98, one hundred acres, to GEORGE PENNEY of Wells for $250.00. This 1797 deed was not entered with Henry Sewall, Kennebec County Register, until April 28, 1814, after George Penney had died. The county records do not reveal how or when Samuel Stewart obtained title to this part of lot no. 98 prior to 1797.

1816   The Kennebec Proprietors sold all of their remaining rights not previously sold to Thomas L. Winthrop and finally closed out their land business here, which had been unprofitable. In turn Thomas L. Winthrop sold one fourth of these rights to James Bridge, one fourth to Reuel Williams, and the remaining half to Joseph H. Williams, Augusta enterprisers. Many of the squatters cleared up the titles to their lands through these new owners.

1817   AMOS BRALEY sold to JOHN PENNEY the south part of lot no. 112 that became the origin of the present Penney farm. The county records do not reveal how Amos Braley acquired his title to this property before this date. The bordering lot no. 4 was sold by Samuel Braley of Belgrade in 1806 to Amos Braley of Readfield for $150.00. In 1799 Samuel Braley bought land in Sidney from John Jones, an employee and representative of the Kennebec Proprietors.